"Jim and Barb have demonstrated for many years their commitment to the restoration of Christian marriages."

Ron Proctor
National Director of Life Builders, Campus Crusade for Christ

"Jim and Barbara have been tested by life. The wisdom they have acquired, and the stories they share in Remember the Rowboats will be of great benefit to anyone who reads it!"

Dr. Robert Lewis
President of LifeReady™ and Founder of Men's Fraternity

"Remember the Rowboats is insightful, biblical, practical, and has tremendous potential to rescue many marriages that are either drifting apart or 'taking on water' and soon may sink. Jim and Barbara, writing from their own personal journey, many years of counseling experience, and a deep belief that God has designed marriage to work well, offer great hope and help. Note especially their Wave makers and Calmers chapter!"

Our Senior Pastor, Pastor Doug Anderson
Calvary Community Church, Williams Bay, WI

"We have co-labored in ministry with Jim and Barbara for almost 8 years and have come to greatly respect their godly marriage. They practice what they preach in this honest and practical book. And, even though my husband and I have been married nearly 30 years and in full-time ministry even longer, God is using their exhortations to cause us to see areas where we may subtly be drifting apart. Our prayer is that you too will grab the ropes that they suggest and begin tying your marital boats!"

Carl and Cyndi Johnson
Staff members with Campus Crusade for Christ for 33 years

"Drifting" in opposite directions, as described by Jim and Barbara, is the archenemy of a strong, long-term marriage. By applying the biblical principles in this book, everyone from newlyweds to seasoned veterans can lay a strong foundation for a closer, more fulfilling and God-honoring marriage."

Karen and Ron Grosse
Lighthouse Christian Books, Green Bay, Wisconsin
Married 43 years

"We use several whole chapters from this book in mentoring couples as well as Men's Fraternity leadership training. The chapters on the Gospel presentation as well as the 7 Ties for your Rowboat are just a few examples of why this book is worth buying, reading, and applying in everyone's marriage whether newlyweds or 40-year veterans like us!"

Darryl and Judy Sheggrud
EncourageMENt Ministries

"Here is a couple who knows a lot about making marriages strong."

Al and Lorraine Broom
Founders of Church Dynamics International

Remember the Rowboats

Anchor your Marriage to Christ

Jim and Barbara Grunseth

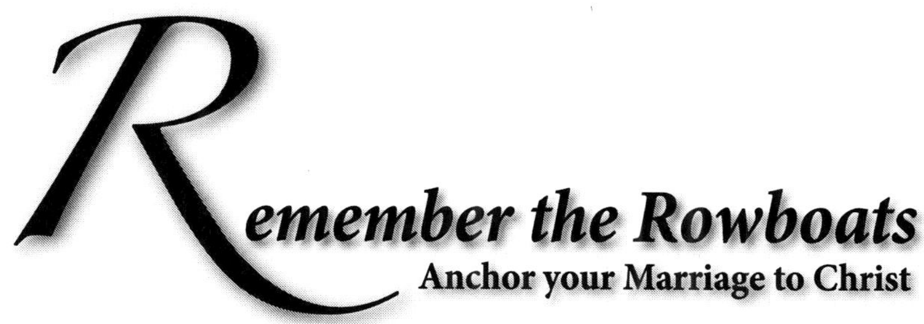

Jim and Barbara Grunseth

River City Press, Inc.
Life Changing Books

Remember the Rowboats

ISBN: 1-934327-40-9
978-1-934327-40-1

Graphic Design & Cover:
Sara Jo Johnson
Vincent Ransom

Editor:
Charlene Meadows
Sara Jo Johnson

Publisher:
River City Press, Inc.
4301 Emerson Avenue North
Minneapolis, MN 55412
www.rivercitypress.net
publisher@rivercitypress.net

Credits and Dedication

Although this book has been in the making for over 8 years, it expresses what God has taught us over a lifetime. It would be impossible to name all the people and references that have played a role in the formation of **Remember the Rowboats.**

We specifically wish to mention and thank Dennis and Barbara Rainey and the entire FamilyLife Team of Campus Crusade for Christ. My (Jim's) years serving with them and, together, our wonderful experiences attending FamilyLife Conferences has contributed much to this material. May God continue to bless them!

We also wish to note the powerful impact and influence Ron and Della Proctor and the Life Builders Team of Campus Crusade for Christ have had on this material. Their emphasis on the **"Faith Principle"** and the vital importance of helping to fulfill our Lord's Great Commission cannot be overstated. May God richly bless them as well.

Don and Sally Merideth, and their book, **Becoming One,** (Thomas Nelson Publishers, New York), must be noted. The biblical principles and their keen insight into human nature as it relates to Christian marriage have been a spring board for some of the ideas in this book such as the problems of "selfishness and performance-based relationships."

We wish to dedicate this book to two wonderful groups of people in our lives. The first group is our small group from church of young couples known as **The Marriage Patriots.** We have field tested these concepts with their major input. They have helped us immensely.

The second group is our seven children, their mates and our precious grandchildren. Sara and her husband Aaron, Alisha, Dan and his wife Jennie, JonVincent, Anne and her husband Ben, Sarah, and Brittney and her husband Adam have blessed us and have had to deal with the great challenges and difficulties of loss in their lives and of blending a very large family. We are indebted to them and thank them for sticking with us.

Jim and Barbara Grunseth

Contents

Drift proof your marriage with lasting hope from God.

How To Use This Book

- **Remember The Rowboats** will have the greatest impact and benefit if it is used in a "Couple to Couple" mentoring setting where two couples meet regularly, in one of their homes. Usually one couple is the Host (Mentoring Couple) and the other couple is the Guest (Mentored Couple). Always both couples need to be committed to becoming further equipped to mentor other couples down the road. (2 Timothy 2:2)

- This material will also be very effective if used in a small group setting. Four to six couples is best. It is wise to enlist an even number of couples, married or engaged. During this small group experience, there will be several times when couples will need to pair off "Couple to Couple" for discussion, interaction, and prayer. Each couple is to read the material assigned and answer the respective Small Group Discussion questions and assignments **prior** to meeting.

- Pastors, church leaders, and Christian counselors will find this material effective in either counseling couples or in training engaged couples for their upcoming marriage and life ministry.

- **A Quiet Place for You to Journal** is the last section of this book. This is designed for the reader to ponder, meditate, and write down thoughts, insights, and reflections. It is to be a quiet and safe retreat for you to express your heart to the Lord.

Jim and Barbara Grunseth

Chapter 1

Green Lake

On a warm August night the water looks black as tea. This night, the moon was full and the breeze gentle. My friend and I were out in the middle of Green Lake, Wisconsin in a rustic boat. The sun had long since set. It was around 10:00 PM.

The fish were not biting so we sat quietly enjoying the silence. The two of us watched the shimmering moonbeams dance across the water's surface. It had been a long time since I had gotten this far away from phones, bills, and traffic. Amazing! I did not quite know how to act or feel. What do you do when you have no demands placed upon you? Oh how I enjoyed the peace and quiet. The calm was very real.

As Brad and I were sitting in our boat, the sound of beautiful choral voices could be heard coming from behind the trees on the shore line about a half mile away. We listened intently. An inner city group had come up from Chicago for the weekend at the old Baptist Church Camp. My imagination got the best of me and I was transported back to somewhere in the 1930's.

Oh the words that traveled across the waters to us! "*What can wash away my sin? Nothing but the blood of Jesus.*" Later they sang "*Amazing Grace, how sweet the sound that saved a wretch like me*". I could have sat in that boat all night listening quietly to the melodies, the frogs, and the gentle lapping of waves against our boat. It was one of those evenings that only comes along once in a great while, sometimes only once in a lifetime. I am glad I was there. God taught me that night.

Drifting

Allow Barbara and me to take you to Green Lake late at night on a summer's eve. All is warm and quiet. You notice two rowboats together out in the middle of the lake. They are indeed together yet neither is anchored and they are not tied together with rope or anything.

As the evening progresses hour after hour, the gentle currents and waves have their natural effect. Slowly, subtly, without trying, the two rowboats gradually begin to drift apart from one another. Inch by inch, foot by foot, distance grows between them. They did not plan on this happening. They wanted to be together, but the natural forces of the lake took over.

At the break of dawn, one boat finds himself bumping up against the dam where muskies are caught. The other boat discovers she has drifted into the shallows at the opposite end of the lake where the lily pads and bullfrogs are. They begin to wonder, "How did you get way over there? What happened? Who are you? Perhaps being with you was a mistake!"

Whatever you do, remember the rowboats! If you don't, your enemy, the devil, will have his way. He will slowly, perhaps over a long period of time, drift you apart from one another. The enemy of your souls is powerful, vicious, and relentless. He will do whatever it takes to keep your marriage and home from being used to "*snatch others from the fire and save them*". (Jude 1:23)

You must remember, "*Be self-controlled and alert. Your enemy the devil prowls around like a roaring lion looking for someone to devour. Resist him, standing firm in the faith, because you know that your brothers throughout the world are undergoing the same kind of sufferings.*" (1 Peter 5:8,9)

He will go to elaborate lengths with precision and attention to detail in order to convince you that you are not the light of the world. Jesus says, "*You are the light of the world... let your light shine before men, that they may see your good deeds and praise your Father in heaven.*" (Taken in part from Matthew 5:14-16)

Unless your marriage is anchored to the Lord Jesus Christ, men, women, and children will suffer torment and hopelessness in Hell's eternity. The devil wants praise for himself. He will do whatever it takes to prevent you from praising your Heavenly Father.

Your marriage is God's loving light to those He loves and longs to rescue from the murky waters of sin and eternal death.

If you have been slowly and subtly drifting apart, please call upon God to save and strengthen your love and marriage. Please read the following letter we received from Debby who is now desperate, broken, and overwhelmed.

Dear Jim and Barbara,

Steve moved out Saturday. I filed for divorce Tuesday. He said in counseling that he wanted a divorce and wanted to be single. I really believe he will renew his relationship with his girlfriend. I told the girls (two little blond-headed sweethearts!) and they were upset.

I bought them a puppy. I can take my grief but theirs is more than I can bear at times. I try to reassure them of their father's love for them but it's just not true. Steve doesn't love anyone. He never spends any time with them. Please pray that somehow Steve will turn back to the love of God he once had.

He has violated his faith so badly though that it will take a real miracle. He has stopped going to church. All he seems to think about is his work, pleasing clients, and going to cocktail parties. Financially, I'm strapped. I don't have a job. I will have to get one.

I'm getting to be quite a prayer warrior. My faith has been so strengthened by this adversity. I know better than ever what it means to cling to Christ. On Christ the solid Rock I stand. All other ground is sinking sand. Pray, please, that I forgive him.

Love,
Debby

Do not let this happen to you! God desires your marriage to be His chosen instrument of hope and oneness to draw to Him the drifting, the drowning, and the discouraged. If couples are left to drift, they won't stand a chance of surviving. They, like neglected boats, will separate, deteriorate, and sink. Understand this: Satan's plan for your marriage is isolation and separation. God's plan for your marriage is oneness and intimacy. What plan are you on?

Small Group Discussion

1. Discuss what you think is meant by Satan's plan for your marriage verses God's plan for your marriage.

2. What battles and struggles do you see today's marriages facing? How do you think they are coping? What do they do to medicate their emotional pain?

3. **(Optional)** What are the tensions and pressures you experience in your marriage? If appropriate, you can share as a group. Only those feeling safe should share. No one should be forced to share or be put on the spot. Sometimes couples will open up with just one other couple. It is up to you. Remember: What is shared in your group stays in your group.

4. Go to the second to the last section of this book entitled, **Wave Makers and Wave Calmers** (page 141).
   During the weeks ahead, pace yourselves as a couple to be sure you begin and finish the **Growth Assignment** (page 142). Your answers will be discussed near the end of this book study. Be sure to have read about every Wave Maker and Wave Calmer and that you each have **circled** one from **each** category that speaks to your heart the most.

5. Please ask for prayer requests and then close in prayer.

Chapter 2

Natural Forces

Imagine quietly resting under a tall pine, on the edge of a large stand of trees. It is late morning on a warm, sunny day. All is still except for the gentle breeze. You look up and see the treetops quietly swaying, softly whispering. You sigh deeply and close your eyes.

As you contemplate the serenity of your surroundings, your attention is soon drawn to the lake's shoreline about 30 feet away. You begin to observe the lake and the natural forces that affect it. Think of the lake as the environment in which you live. Like two rowboats, you and your mate are at the mercy of the environment unless you have a plan and you both work diligently at it.

There are pressures and forces at work in your marriage that will affect your relationship and the relationships you come in contact with. Pressures will naturally and gradually wear down the sweetness, and health of your relationship. Earlier, you would not keep apart. Soon, you do not mind being apart. Later on, you look forward to being apart. Unless equipped, your marriage loyalties will wane. Most of the time, these forces lead your marriage through four stages we call the **Devil's Ladder**. The Lord, however, has a sure plan for your marriage, the **Lord's Ladder.**

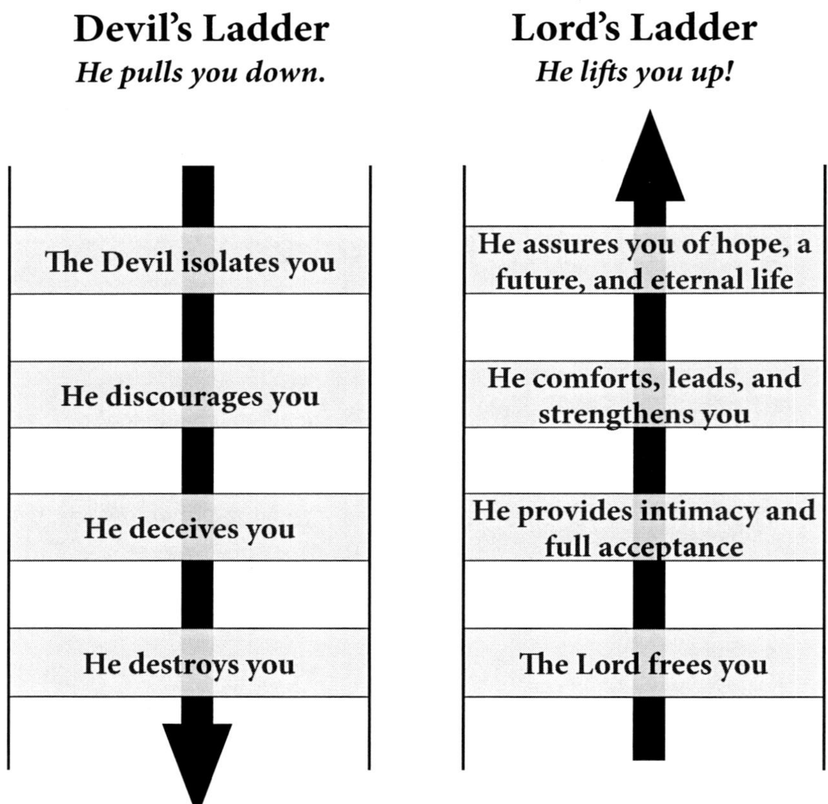

According to Galatians Chapter 5, marriage partners will either choose to live by faith or they will choose to be controlled by their flesh. The first will bring hope, oneness, and life. The second will bring despair, isolation, and death.

Memorize this:

"Faith is choosing to live as though the Bible is true, regardless of circumstances, emotions, or cultural trends."

Life Builders Faith Principle, Campus Crusade for Christ

If one does not live by faith, and consequently love by faith then the flesh rules and the wages of sin is death. The marriage that refuses to live by faith will eventually become unhealthy, unhappy, and unfruitful.

Know your Enemy! Be aware of the spiritual battle you are in. (Study Ephesians Chapter 6: 10-18) The devil has a plan to destroy your marriage.

Be sure you are constantly aware of the **Devil's Ladder** and the **Lord's Ladder.** Warn other couples of the dangers and warning signs of the first one and also the blessings and joy of the second one. Marriage partners who fall into deep sin, or who file for divorce are **pulled** down the Devil's Ladder rung by rung. He is a master at greasing the rungs. Help others to see this and to get off that ladder! (Ezekiel 33:1-6)

Choose to cling to the Lord Jesus and His wonderful ladder. Most assuredly, He will **lift** you and your marriage up. Ask Him to do this. Seek Him together with all your heart. He will never fail you or the marriage He has called you to.

Waves Push You Apart

On the lake, two rowboats are meant to be together. They are initially close but as the waves have their constant, subtle effect, the boats slowly drift away from one another. When a couple marries, the last thing on their minds is isolation and rejection. They would never expect, as mates, to naturally grow apart to the point of breaking their vows. Differing backgrounds, family experiences, and past relationships are like waves. If you do not prepare for their influence and impact, you and your boats might take in some water!

Many such boats are not at all equipped for the waves that will inevitably ensue. Likewise, couples often flounder, and drift apart when life's waves crash up against them. When Barbara and I got married we were not prepared for differences we encountered. Boy, were we caught off guard!

Jim's roots come from northern Wisconsin, good Norwegian and German stock. His dad came from eleven brothers and sisters and worked a farm, general store, and the post office for a town of 99 people. There was plenty of love, homemade breads, pies, and swimming holes. For many years indoor plumbing was only something you saw in the Sears catalog. There was no hint of finer culture.

Jim writes, "Mom, as German as they come, believed in three square meals a day. 'You must have some meat and something sweet at every meal' she would say. Dad was a principal of middle and elementary schools in Elkhorn for over 37 years. I experienced sort of a double life being "the principal's son". Most of the teachers loved me and many of the boys in class picked on me. I did not like school at all.

My older brother, John, seldom let me play wiffle ball with him and his friends. I seemed to always be the little brother tag along who just got in the way.

Mom comforted and fed. Dad provided and told us what to do. We never had more than one car. We only had two bedrooms. We enjoyed food so much; we could have an engaging talk on the qualities of certain acclaimed cheeseburgers from Art and Sylvia's Diner across town."

Barbara, the oldest of 5 children, grew up on the North Shore of Chicago in the town of Deerfield. She writes, "My father, uncle, and grandpa owned and operated a successful heating and cooling business. My German, Norwegian, and Polish heritage included frequent participation in and a genuine appreciation for music and the fine arts. My mom, grandma, and I loved visiting Orchestra Hall in Chicago as well as the Goodman Theatre and Art Institute. I was the concert mistress in my high school orchestra. I thoroughly enjoyed my school experience.

My family and I were involved in everything from piano and baseball, to hockey and horseback riding. My three younger brothers and sister and I enjoyed going to the country club to golf, swim, play tennis or just sit and read and enjoy great food and refreshments.

My mom developed the reputation for being a very hard worker. You can imagine with that many children! She was a great teacher and fed her brood well! We frequently had friends over for parties or after school treats. Fine hospitality was modeled for me at an early age.

Our family summer lake home in Wisconsin offered a gorgeous setting for vacation. There were sail boats, rowboats, speedboats, and water skiing, fishing, picnicking, cookouts, and hammocks. My brothers, sister, and I were often busy floating on air mattresses and tubes, or attempting new dives off the pier. I fondly remember us standing real still in the water to let the minnows tickle our feet. What riotous fun it was! We spent warm days searching the beach for smooth stones to skip on the water. We also discovered crayfish and bull heads under the beached rowboat. Other times we would hunt for and spy lost or discarded lake treasures that would wash up on shore."

Weather Erodes Your Timbers

Remember the last time you were at water's edge? If you looked closely, you might have seen driftwood, a broken piece of glass, seaweed, and perhaps part of an old rope washed up on shore. The sun, the storms, and temperature changes do their work. It is a known fact that water, over time, is one of the most erosive elements on earth.

Barbara and I were raised differently. We approach life from different angles. We also developed different styles of parenting. Since we each had been married once before, we had rather different views of married life, conflict resolution, and finances. Barbara is merciful, gentle, yet firm. I, however, went to West Point and had instilled in me discipline, punctuality, and respect for rules. Needless to say, we had to make some serious adjustments and compromises. We learned to pray at bedtime every night together. This is the best decision we ever made!

There is a reason why people secure their boats, batten down the hatches, and anchor them well before the storm comes. If they do not, the storm would damage their craft and possibly smash it into other boats or the pier. Do you have a plan to batten down the hatches and secure well your marriage against the inevitable storms of life? If you do not, you will end up listing, smashed, or at the bottom of the lake. Most marriages are clueless.

Small Leaks Can Sink You

Our son, Dan, took Barbara and me fishing on a small, private pond one day in Northern Indiana. The water was clean, the fish plentiful, and the company enjoyable. We actually caught some good-sized fish! However, there were several small problems. In the back of this rustic, aging rowboat, I noticed 3 or 4 nickel-sized holes in the watery floor. While Dan and Barbara were having great fun catching fish, I was watching arcs of water shooting up 5 or 6 inches into the boat. Laughably, I tried to plug up a hole or two with my now soaked tennis shoes. The more I tried to stop the incoming water, the more water seemed to rush into the boat. The boat was filling fast.

So what did I do? Of course, I tried to stand up in order to get a better picture of the situation. Wrong thing to do! With 5 inches of water in the rowboat, stability is something only to hope for. If it had not been for smart thinking on Barbara's part, all of us would have joined our fish friends in the pond. As it was, our boat almost did not make it back to shore.

Two small, steady leaks that naturally occur in marriage are:

1. **Self-centeredness**

2. **The performance-based relationship**

These two must be faced and dealt with on a daily basis. Why should the devil wade out into the lake of your marriage and devote time, personnel, and energy, if you and your mate are willing to destroy your relationship all on your own?

Take a look at self-centeredness. You must decide that holiness and selflessness before the Lord is that which determines your happiness. You must resolve that obedience to God is the entrance gate to the pleasures He intends for you. Ask the Lord to instill in you a healthy fear of God. Ask Him to reveal to you anything in your life, your home, or on your property that erodes a pure lifestyle, or offends His Holiness. Finally, you both must submit to a Christ-centered way of life where grace, thankfulness, and mercy abound. Asking for forgiveness and then forgiving one another should be a common theme in your home. The devil can tamper with many things, but these he cannot touch. Where Jesus resides, the devil must retreat.

James 4:7-10 reads, "[7]***Submit*** *yourselves, then, to God.* ***Resist*** *the devil, and he will flee from you.* [8]***Come near*** *to God and he will come near to you.* ***Wash*** *your hands, you sinners, and* ***purify*** *your hearts, you double-minded.* [9]***Grieve,*** *mourn and wail.* ***Change*** *your laughter to mourning and your joy to gloom.* [10]***Humble*** *yourselves before the Lord, and he will lift you up.*" (Bold added for emphasis) Make these choices and just watch what God does!

Self-centeredness is pride unleashed and self-focus gone bad. It is our ugly attempt at getting what we want and what we think we deserve. It is putting our self ahead of others. It is getting our needs met through sinful, inappropriate means. Remember, the self-centered heart is always unsatisfied. Discontentment is the fragrance of the self-centered. It is carnal and dark and wholly opposed to God and His Holy Word, the Bible. It is the devil's delight! God's marriage will be destroyed if this is not dealt a deathblow on a daily basis.

The Apostle Paul, addressing the Christians in Rome warned them:

"In the same way, count yourselves dead to sin but alive to God in Christ Jesus. Therefore do not let sin reign in your mortal body so that you obey its evil desires. Do not offer the parts of your body to sin, as instruments of wickedness, but rather offer yourselves to God, as those who have been brought from death to life; and offer the parts of your body to him as instruments of righteousness. For sin shall not be your master, because you are not under law, but under grace." (Romans 6:11-14)

If sin is your master, and not Jesus, your marriage will breed pain and death. If you are making provisions for the flesh, the devil will lie to you. He will whisper, "Of course this choice is sinful, yet full of pleasure. Yes, there will be feelings of self-loathing, guilt, shame, and condemnation, but you will quickly get over it and your sin will only hurt you." The truth is this: If you choose sin, you will not get over it quickly and others will always suffer. Always.

If God convicts you of a sinful, self-centered heart where pride, lust, discontentment, anger, or unforgiveness are frequent guests, confess your sin, turn from your wicked ways, and ask Jesus to take control of the throne of your life.

In the New Testament, John writes,

"If we confess our sins, he is faithful and just and will forgive us our sins and purify us from all unrighteousness." (1 John 1:9)

We are finding in our lives what helps is to remember to:

- **Spend regular, quality time with the Lord Jesus and His Word, the Bible**
- **Stay off His throne**
- **Do what He says**

You see, until you and your mate decide to start wanting what God wants for your life and marriage more than what you personally want, your marriage will be of no great threat to Satan. His scheme to enslave souls and secure them in the stench and drudgery of endless darkness will continue.

Now take a look at the performance-based relationship. If this small leak is not dealt with immediately, its nickel-sized hole will lead to the sinking of your boat! Whenever you choose to take control of your life and prevent the Lord Jesus His rightful place on the throne of your heart, you become what the Bible calls carnal, worldly, or in the flesh. So if you are not Spirit-filled (by faith), then you are controlled by your flesh. Discord, impatience, and dissatisfaction will permeate your life in much the same way as rotting fish smell permeates a shoreline. When your flesh controls you, you will always base your relationships on performance.

The Apostle Paul in Galatians 5:16-18 says, *"So I say, live by the Spirit, and you will not gratify the desires of the sinful nature. For the sinful nature desires what is contrary to the Spirit, and the Spirit what is contrary to the sinful nature. They are in conflict with each other, so that you do not do what you want. But if you are led by the Spirit, you are not under law."*

You know you are in a performance-based relationship if you feel you have to earn another person's favor or love. It looks like this: "Honey, I will love you, care for you, and cherish you when you measure up to my standards of performance." Love that must be earned is never love! It is **conditional probation** in which the person wanting to be loved always feels that if he or she does not perform up to standards, they will experience some form of rejection, shame, or even punishment. This demonic perversion is from the pit of Hell. This type of relationship is utterly foreign to our loving Heavenly Father. What happens in the performance-based relationship is deadly. Invariably, the person seeking to be loved and accepted strives futilely to earn the right to be favored or treasured. But as soon as the "other" person notices the effort, the bar is raised. The poor soul seeking acceptance is crushed in defeat. This terrible cycle continues until the death of the relationship.

Sunk!

Small Group Discussion — Chapter 2

1. How have your different backgrounds affected your relationship?

2. How exposed were you to the problems of self-centeredness and performance-based relationships in the homes you grew up in? (Note: There will be no blaming of parents or grudge holding towards them. This is simply so you more clearly understand rooted, generational problems in your own lives that need to be dealt with.)

3. Without mentioning names, how do you see self-centeredness and performance-based relationships affecting other couples you know? (Again, no names please.)

4. Discuss the differences between the Devil's Ladder and the Lord's Ladder. Why do you think "**Isolation**" is central to the devil's strategies to destroy relationships?

5. **(Optional)** How have your own self-centeredness and performance-based issues affected your relationships? In what ways have you required your loved one to improve or measure up before you bestow love and favor?

6. Please ask for prayer requests and then close in prayer.

Chapter 3

Jim's Rowboat Story

Although I became a Christian at 18, I did not really get serious about the Lord until much later. As a young husband and father, my family suffered because I was carnal and double minded. I wanted to follow God but I also craved the respect and approval of people. My priorities were out of balance and sin had its hold on me. We were all fairly miserable. I regret those sins. God began to humble me and break down my pride in my late 20's. Soon after I turned 30, I renewed my vows to the Lord and committed to full time, vocational ministry.

Five years later, we moved to Illinois so I could attend seminary. The moving van that we hired to transport all of our belongings went up in flames during some repair work. We were lied to and cheated by this moving company. It took three years to get it settled. This crisis took up much of my time during my first year of seminary.

At the beginning of my final year of school, Julie was diagnosed with lupus, sojgrens syndrome, and, worst of all, advanced breast cancer. It was as if our hopes, plans, and dreams, were crystal figurines being smashed by a brutal sledgehammer. No matter how you look at it, cancer is an awful and sadistic disease. It not only eats away at the person it is ravaging, but it also eats away at the whole family. Relationships are strained. Emotions become wooden and empty. Anger and fear become the norm. Exhaustion is standard. Cancer lives with you.

Through eight surgeries, four regimens of chemotherapy, three separate hair losses, and months in hospitals, a frightening bone marrow transplant, and five unsuccessful trips to Bethesda, Maryland (National Cancer Institute), Julie fought her disease with courage maintaining her faith in God. Many were strengthened by her bravery. The chemotherapy helped to extend her life but it was devastating to her and to the rest of us.

She suffered from severe depression at times and experienced terrible mood swings that made living in our home difficult. On a regular basis, she would cycle into a destructive, violent rage. Other times she could be very pleasant. Then, when least expected, her mood would change and she would beat, kick, and claw me. I should have called 911 and gotten her help many times. But I failed to do so.

You see I was trying to protect and preserve our image as the wonderful, suffering missionary family. Worse, I resisted getting her professional help because, deep inside, I thought the town's people and church family would think I was a bad husband. I thought if I were the husband God wanted me to be, Julie would respond with grace, kindness, and a stable emotional frame of mind. She suffered from a bi-polar disorder of some type. Her extended family refused to believe that she was mentally unstable. I begged them for help. My pleas fell on deaf ears.

Frequently, our home was filled with chaos, tension, and anger outbursts. One minute she would be stable and the next she would fall apart. The four kids and I, along with Julie, were on one big roller coaster.

On top of all this, I felt utterly helpless. I was with Julie almost constantly for seven years during this battle, but I could not help her. I could not heal her. The Lord knows I tried just about everything known to man. The suspense of not knowing when the cancer would strike again or take her life was like swimming in dark waters with that shark from "Jaws" near us.

We could never escape its presence or its influence. I once described living with long term cancer in our family as living with an evil, vindictive presence holding all of us hostage. Even when we went on vacation, "it" came with us. It controlled the life of our family. It was a cruel and terrifying time.

We put our trust in the Lord but the stress of seeing my wife and the mother of my children slowly melt away like a popsicle on a hot day, gnawed at me relentlessly. I developed severe migraine headaches that lasted 24 hours a day for two years. The pain wrestled me to the floor many times. I became depressed and exhausted, weary beyond words. My heart became like wood. Life to me had the taste of sawdust. I felt old.

I got hooked on prescription painkillers. It was like I could not get through the continuous headache pain without them. I prayed and prayed but they would not go away. I had bottled up so much agony. You see, I was Julie's husband and father of four children. I felt it was my responsibility to protect my family. Yet I could not stop the cancer.

I sought the Lord and asked several men to meet with me regularly to encourage me, pray with me, and hold me accountable. This was of great help! I confess that several times during the cancer battle, I lost hope. Seven years is a long time. Several times, I felt that God had abandoned me. Thank heavens, I knew this not to be true since Jesus promised to never leave nor forsake me. I was able to put my trust in "what is written" in the Word of God instead of my emotions or my experience. Once again, here is the Faith Definition:

Faith is choosing to live as though the Bible is true, regardless of circumstances, emotions, or cultural trends.

Julie died at home where she wanted to be with all of her family near her. She could no longer breathe since the cancer had invaded her lungs. The morphine and oxygen weren't helping anymore. She told me she wanted to go home to be with Jesus. And on that mid June afternoon, she did. We would have been married twenty years, missing our anniversary by only seven days.

1. Discuss the impact the definition of **Faith** might have on your lives and relationships this week. (i.e.: You might feel today like you are a real loser, but God's Word says "*…you are precious and honored in my sight*" – Isaiah 43:4a. Which will you embrace today?)

   (i.e.: Today you also might believe you are condemned and doomed because of your mistakes, but God's Words tells you, "*Therefore, there is now no condemnation for those who are in Christ Jesus*," Romans 8:1. Which is true? What's it going to be? Knowing the truth is one thing. Loving the truth is quite another. If you choose to love God's truth, you will embrace it and apply it.)

2. Take turns voluntarily sharing your own personal rowboat stories. Place no pressure on anyone to do this. The others in the group should tenderly and supportively listen. Don't try to fix or change. Just love them with your listening ears. If appropriate, perhaps ask the person if it would be OK for someone to pray for them after they have shared. Some in the group might benefit from writing down the story in a personal journal.

3. If possible, have each couple go off to be alone together to ask each other the following **Bridge Builder** question. Let your partner share while you listen attentively. When they are done, say to them the **Four Magic Words: "Please tell me more"**, and then listen lovingly again. Don't fix, don't

correct, and don't disagree. Just listen attentively. Prize them. If time permits, summarize back to your partner what you believe you heard them say. In doing this, you demonstrate that you listened and that you value them. Then reverse roles and repeat the listening and sharing process.

Here is your first **Bridge Builder** question:

Thinking back, what was the most uplifting, memorable time of our relationship?

4. Please ask for prayer requests and then close in prayer.

Chapter 4

Barbara's Rowboat Story

My heart skipped a beat as a surge of adrenaline was released into my system. My husband and I had gone to a company pool party with our three, young children. I was in the living room attending to our four month old, Sarah. I walked into the kitchen to get some water and was met with a crushing blow. My husband and another woman were at the refrigerator locked in a passionate embrace.

My flesh and the Holy Spirit began to war determining the reaction I would choose. I felt rage, shame, betrayal, disbelief, fear, and gut wrenching pain. I turned and walked out in order to sort through all the emotion.

Could it be my marriage of almost ten years was a target of our archenemy, Satan? I recalled the wife of a co-worker warning me to get my husband out of this company before it was too late. Was it now too late?

I prayed for wisdom and strength for battle. I confronted my husband that night in the privacy of our own home. He could not pray with me. His eyes lacked life. They were like deep, dark, cesspools. I cried out, "Abba Father," as I held on to his limp hands. I felt ripped in half as I cried deep, convulsive sobs. I pleaded with God to restore our marriage. Over the next three months I began searching for help. I tried a marriage counselor, but my husband refused to go in to see him, insisting it was all my fault.

I tried new clothes, new feminine manipulations, and pretended to be interested in all my husband's worldly interests. I remember going out with him one night to a series of night clubs he had discovered with his co-workers. I sat there nursing my cocktail watching the people on the dance floor I had just left. Their faces did not reflect deep contentment and the fun times my husband had described.

Just at that moment, the thought came to me; What if the Lord returned right now? My Savior would find me trying to please my husband more than please Him. I asked to be taken home and never went back.

Another night my husband took me to a company party at a private home. After swimming and socializing awhile, I was hungry. I went to the kitchen to the buffet. Food tasted great. The problem was I began to feel very strange. When I made it to the couch, I was relieved to put my head down. Several men came over with my husband and hovered above me. I didn't know at the time but they were into wife swapping.

My husband told the men to leave me alone. It was at that point I recalled Sodom and Gomorrah and I jumped up, ran out the front door, down the street, crying. My husband came after me in the car, took me home, and went back to the party.

During my quiet times with Jesus, His still small voice kept saying, "Let him go." I was so caught up in performing in order to please my husband that I ignored the voice of my Lord. Finally, His words to me were confirmed by two pastors from different states both sharing 1 Corinthians 5:4,5:

"When you are assembled in the name of our Lord Jesus and I am with you in spirit and the power of our Lord Jesus is present, hand this man over to Satan, so that the sinful nature may be destroyed and his spirit saved on the day of the Lord."

I asked my husband to forgive me for not being the wife he thought he needed and again pledged my commitment to him and to our Lord. My husband chose to divorce not only his wife and three children, but also everything and everybody involved with Jesus.

He took all the money out of the bank and turned off all utilities in the house. I prayed prostrate on the floor for God's leading. He provided me with a childcare job for some wealthy people. God was always faithful to supply all our needs.

I saw thirty four marriages dissolved that memorable day in court, all due to the devil's ultimate lie: irreconcilable differences. God was merciful to me and answered my prayer to remove me from the city and state we were living in. I could not bear to watch my husband in the clutches of the enemy.

The children and I set up house keeping near my family in Wisconsin. I was physically drained, emotionally rent in half, and spiritually exhausted from the battle. I determined to batten down the hatches and pull my children close to ward off any further destruction of our family unit.

Jesus became my husband. I ran to His arms daily for answers through prayer and His Word. I had a lot of fear at first. All responsibility seemed to rest on me. But I knew my enemy and I knew how to use the Word of God as a weapon.

When I had panic attacks at the grocery store or driving a car, I would set my mind on specific scriptures. I was in a war between the flesh and the Spirit.

"You will keep in perfect peace him whose mind is steadfast, because he trusts in you." (Isaiah 26:3)

"Do not conform any longer to the pattern of this world, but be transformed by the renewing of your mind. Then you will be able to test and approve what God's will is—his good, pleasing and perfect will." (Romans 12:2)

"Set your minds on things above, not on earthly things. For you died, and your life is now hidden with Christ in God." (Colossians 3:2, 3)

I prayed that I would not have to work at a job outside the home until my one year old was in first grade. I wanted to be the one to raise my children in those formative years to honor and glorify the Lord. He honored my heart's cry by allowing me enough in savings and child support to care for our needs.

After Sarah's fifth birthday, I was offered three teaching jobs, one of which was at a Christian school. My children and I were there for twelve years.

I told the Lord long ago, that I would never again go out "looking" for a man to marry. If He wanted me to marry again, He would have to bring across my path a Christian man, proven to be faithful. We would both need to sense God's irrevocable calling to marriage and would need to compliment each other's ministry to advance the Kingdom of God.

1. Continue taking turns voluntarily sharing your own personal rowboat stories. Place no pressure on anyone to do this. The others in the group should tenderly and supportively listen. Don't try to fix or change. Just love them with your listening ears. If appropriate, perhaps ask the person if it would be OK for someone to pray for them after they have shared.

2. If possible, have each couple go off to be alone together to ask each other the following **Bridge Builder** question. Let your partner share while you listen attentively. When they are done, say to them the **Four Magic Words: "Please tell me more"**, and then listen lovingly again. Don't fix, don't correct, and don't disagree. Just listen attentively. Prize them. If time permits, summarize back to your partner what you believe you heard them say. In doing this, you demonstrate that you listened and that you value them. Then reverse roles and repeat the listening and sharing process.

Here is your second **Bridge Builder** question:

When do you feel loved, valued, affirmed, or respected by me the most?

3. Please ask for prayer requests and then close in prayer.

Chapter 5

The Storm

When I was 16 our church youth group set out from Milwaukee to cross Lake Michigan on a ferry clipper ship. Oh the fun and adventure of it all! It would almost be like being out on the high seas! I had seen enough pirate and swashbuckler movies to know that heroes and courageous souls always went to sea to fight against evil and the rigorous challenge of the ocean elements. Being more of a romantic at the time and possessing a vivid imagination, I thought a little rough weather on Lake Michigan would be exciting.

The first half an hour of our ferryboat ride was smooth and calm. Suddenly, the sky grew dark, the wind picked up, and the temperature dropped about 20 degrees. I thought, "Hey, just like the movies!" I began to whisper to myself, "Eye me buckos! Shivar me timbers! Yo ho, yo ho! A Pirate's life far me!"

All in all, I was having a great time. The other kids in our group, however, were not as thrilled as I was. Even the crew's faces turned gray and deadpan. I knew we were in trouble when the waves reached 15 feet in height and the sky was black as tar. Within minutes, 75 % of crew and passengers were on the floor or in the bathrooms seasick. A few hearty souls including myself were the only ones not crawling. We quickly got blankets, crackers and lemons and started getting people secure and stabilized. One guy was so sick he was almost unconscious on the open deck. He easily could have washed overboard. He was soaked and sick. We found him just in time. I realized it would be by the hand of God that we would make it back to the landing dock at Milwaukee. Eventually, we did! Now I possess a healthy respect for storms and water.

Remember the last storm that hit your life? It may have approached you slowly or descended upon you without warning. Storms in the form of troubles, trials, and difficulties are inevitable.

When my first wife of 20 years died, I was left with 4 children, a son and three daughters. I had watched Julie slowly die for 7 years. That coupled with her emotional battles forced me to grieve the loss of her before she actually passed away. I call it pre-death grieving. On the other hand, Julie's family and my children were grieving differently. They started most of their grief process the day she died. The Monday after the Saturday funeral, I fell apart. All the friends and relatives had left for home and I was alone. I finally had the nerve to open the small burgundy velvet bag that the funeral director had given me. In it were all of Julie's rings. It all hit me like a train. She was gone. I lost it. I fell to my bedroom floor on all fours and began to sob and wail. I cried with such groaning I thought I might pass out. Even though I had many years to prepare for this loss, nothing could have prepared me for the shear bluntness of her death and funeral.

Being impatient and quite impulsive, I wanted and desperately needed to get on with my life. I could not stand being single. I felt like a fish out of water. Although the last 7 years were at best hellish, I had a strong love for the institution of marriage. I knew God had made me in such a way that it was not good for this man to be alone! I was in deep crisis.

Several months later, I went over to Julie's parent's house to let them know, honorably, that I was ready to start dating again. I figured it would be best if they heard it from me directly than from some gossiper. My meeting with her parents did not go well. Julie's dad blew up, stood up and looked at me eye to eye. Her mom began to cry and looked at me as if I were a traitor, or a monster. My oldest child, Sara, became so nervous, she ran to the bathroom to throw up from all the tension. I had to quickly leave for fear that a fistfight might ensue.

Much vicious gossip started throughout our small hometown. I was called "Satan" to my face. By others, I was told to, "Go to Hell!" I confess my anger burned against these people whom I had loved for 23 years. What right did they have to try to run my life or dictate who or when I marry?

I was told that I had my shot at marriage and now that period of my life was over. My role in life was to serve the kids and that was it. I felt people were trying to control me and thus control my children. I refused to let that happen. Certain people turned on me.

Every night on my knees I cried out to God, "I know I don't deserve this, but Lord, I am begging you for mercy!" I actually went through the Bible and did a complete Hebrew and Greek word study on the word “mercy”. I now know begging God is a wonderful thing. Only the heart that is destitute can beg. He heard my feeble cries and gave me more than what I prayed for. He literally brought Barbara to me. My Prayer Partner, Tim, had a dream about Barbara. He and Sue, his wife, believed God would have them mention her to me. I called her, having no idea of her appearance. We chatted for 2 hours and I fell madly in love with her.

Key people previously close to my family began systematically turning my children against me. Lies were told. My oldest rebelled, left, and moved in with a relative. Slanderous calls were made to churches I worked with in ministry in an attempt to stop our marriage. I also received 5 letters about 5 days apart from relatives on my in-law’s side berating me and pleading with me not to marry Barbara. Each letter was so filled with guilt, shame, and condemnation that he who inspired them had to be the devil, “The Accuser of the Brethren.” One Christian friend told me I could not marry Barbara because she was divorced material. I guess this man failed to understand that it was her husband who divorced her against her pleadings and he was now on his third wife!

Barbara recalls her storm began with her marriage of 10 years ending. “As the single parent of three young children, I was responsible for all the workings of the family. I did not feel equipped for that. I had to focus on the essentials and eliminate the unnecessary. I learned to die to lots of dreams. The Lord taught me to live in the moment, not in the past or the future. Consequently, all my energy was spent each day meeting the needs as they arose. I leaned heavily on the Lord in prayer. The devil lied to me often and I would pace back and forth shouting Scripture truths at him.

Most people thought I had given up and had my priorities wrong. Why wasn't I looking for a man to help me and take care of me? Why was I settling for such a low income and quiet life style? It was awkward to socialize with married couples and their children. A single woman can be threatening. My children and I became very comfortable and felt protected in our routine existence centered on the Lord in our cottage by the lake. I taught at Faith Christian School where my children attended. The faculty and families were very supportive. We began many lasting, God ordained friendships there. Then one day, I received a call from Jim.

God does not waste one life experience. He continually gives us opportunities to become more like His Son through the testing of our faith. At 43 years of age was I up for another family challenge? After eleven years of single parenting, could I handle four more children?

I recalled a Scripture God reminded me of often that had proven to be true in my life. 2 Corinthians 1:3,4:

"Praise be to the God and Father of our Lord Jesus Christ, the Father of compassion and the God of all comfort, who comforts us in all our troubles, so that we can comfort those in any trouble with the comfort we ourselves have received from God."

God had comforted me in my times alone with Him. I felt called by Him to comfort others, specifically Jim and his kids. Jim won my heart by making me feel like I was treasured and cherished. We were ready for the call to marriage and all the difficulties we would face, with the Holy Spirit to guide us.

Holidays were particularly challenging. Since Jim and I married, our holidays became focused on who showed up instead of the purpose of the celebration. Jim feared the holidays and I struggled. Most of the time, his three daughters did not come for the party. Sometimes they made a showing but only after they had their best of times with their mom's relatives. Jim felt like those relatives were stealing his kids. He felt betrayed.

He tried to enter into our celebrations but inevitably would end up depressed with a migraine headache. I tried to include him and his kids in our traditions and make the Lord the central focus, but somehow it never worked.

My blood relations got tired of the drama. They began to back away from the situation. My children struggled with the loss of quality time with mom. They began to withdraw into their separate worlds pursuing their own studies and interests."

When we attempted to blend our families, all of our kids were either in or approaching the teen years. The ages of my children at that time were 18, 16, 12, and 10. Barbara's children were 17, 14, and 11. Trying to blend two families with teenagers is challenging enough without the backdrop of all this small town hatred, grudge holding, and relentless family drama. We had many strikes against us but Barbara and I decided early on that the Lord Jesus Christ was on our side and that He was enough.

Trust us! There is no such thing as a blended family! We were and still are a "blending" family. It would be like having one family from the State of Maine and a family from Uruguay coming to live together under one roof. We had two completely different backgrounds, two different parenting styles, two views on discipline, curfews, dating, even food! It was the tempest versus teatime. It was like the tortoise and the hare living together. We had to learn to sacrifice our own desires for the betterment of the group. Some understood this. Others fought tooth and nail. We were reminded of what the Apostle Paul said in Ephesians 5:1,2:

"Be imitators of God, therefore, as dearly loved children and live a life of love, just as Christ loved us and gave himself up for us as a fragrant offering and sacrifice to God."

We chose to allow nothing to erode or weaken our devotion to Christ. We did not give in to threats, demonic attacks, bad dreams, rejection, or hatred. We clung to Christ and His Word. Barbara and I held hands and prayed out loud together often to nurture and protect our marriage. Although I battle feelings of failure regarding my role as dad, I am learning to forget the past and give my burdens and failures to Jesus one at a time. Through such loss and injustice, we are learning Christ's character qualities of humility, forgiveness, and forbearance. We are working at making our home God's loving, restoring lighthouse to our children and the world.

Small Group Discussion Chapter 5

1. Discuss the following question: "Have you ever experienced a very painful or difficult experience in your life? If people feel safe, ask them to share their experience with the group. What feelings and emotions were experienced?

2. In what ways do broken or lost relationships affect you and your marriage?

3. Have the group discuss why betraying a loved one is so hurtful and destructive. What does it feel like to be betrayed, threatened, or slandered?

4. Why is it painful and destructive if one marital partner tampers with his or her vows and begins to share devotion with someone outside the marriage including pornography? This is devotion that was promised solely to their mate at the marriage alter. Remember the devil is a master at setting traps and snaring you and your mate. What does it mean to **Guard your heart and guard your marriage?**

5. What emotions do you think Jesus experienced when He was betrayed?

6. If possible, have each couple go off to be alone together to ask each other the following **Bridge Builder** question. Let your partner share while you listen attentively. When they are done, say to them the **Four Magic Words: "Please tell me more"**, and then listen lovingly again. Don't fix, don't correct, and don't disagree. Just listen attentively. Prize them. If time permits, summarize back to your partner what you believe you heard them say. In doing this, you demonstrate that you listened and that you value them. Then reverse roles and repeat the listening and sharing process.

Here is your third **Bridge Builder** question:

What has been the most treasured gift that I have given you and why?

7. Please ask for prayer requests and then close in prayer.

Chapter 6

Rules of the Carnal Family

Have you ever gone camping when the weather did not cooperate? A few years back Barbara and I spoke at a wonderful Christian camp up in the northwestern part of Wisconsin. It was a weekend marriage retreat and we had a great time. The people were friendly, the food was good, and the lodging was clean and cozy. This church camp was constructed right near the shoreline of a fairly large lake.

The month was November and on Saturday, the second day of the retreat, the weather turned on us. The wind picked up to 30 to 50 miles per hour. The temperature dropped to below freezing. And cold, slushy sleet and wet snow began to come down. The only problem was, since it was so windy, this frozen mess hit us sideways. It was both difficult and miserable just to walk from one building to another.

I remember looking out on the lake and all I could see was a depressing, grayish green. I could not find where the water stopped and the skyline took over. If you have ever walked in a sideways pelting sleet storm, you will never forget it! Thankfully we had warm cabins to escape to. Anybody staying in a tent would just have to give it up.

Living in or marrying into a carnal family is about as pleasant and rewarding as standing outside in a miserable storm like the one just described. A carnal family is where Christ is forbidden to run the show. This family is not neglectful or purposefully hurtful. This is one in which the family members refuse to cooperate with the Lord Jesus Christ. A carnal family is one where the key influencers absolutely refuse to allow Christ His rightful rule and authority over their home and family.

The carnal family refuses to live by faith. Once again, the definition of faith that we find most useful is this: **Faith is choosing to live as though the Bible is true, regardless of circumstances, emotions, or cultural trends.** This lifestyle is both foreign and unacceptable especially to the carnal family leaders. Why? Living by faith would require them to humble themselves under the mighty hand of God and surrender their will to the Lord Jesus Christ.

Because the carnal family refuses to live by faith, there is a stubborn rejection of anything to do with submitting to the authority of God's Word. The key family influencers may be nice people generally yet they will never relinquish control of their family members. They will never subject their unwritten rules to the light of Christ. There is usually an extended family network that supports this unhealthy, ungodly family system.

Rules Regarding Lines of Authority

Unfortunately we have found that carnal families have some things in common. First, family blood is far more important than the shed blood of Christ. The Word of God is held with little or no reverence. There is usually a matriarchal or patriarchal system of authority. Depending on the fleshly, sinful grip by the one calling the shots, certain key family appointed figures are not to be messed with or disagreed with. Family respect is wonderful but when rulings and edicts coming down from the top are contrary to Scripture, the devil has a hay day!

The leading and next in line patriarchs or matriarchs are entrenched until either they die or just mellow out at the rest home. Then somebody in the extended family will have been groomed to sort of take over ruling authority. There are no ceremonies or speeches. This is all done subconsciously, silently.

Rules Regarding Conduct

These rules come in the form of unwritten and unspoken family bloodline rules passed down from generation to generation. Here is a brief list. It is not exhaustive nor do they always show up in every carnal home.

1. The number one rule is: **Never break the rules!** If you do you will be singled out, marginalized, possibly ostracized, and then punished. If you are blood related, you might be lightly shunned for a while. If non-blood related or simply not a part of the family camp, most likely you will be shunned and punished with sharp and sometimes ruthless revenge.

2. The ruling person has **final authority** and is never to be questioned or challenged. His opinion overrules even God's! Family blood and values trump Christ's shed blood and the Bible.

3. There is the **"No Talk"** rule. This means that we don't share our problems within our family and for sure no one outside the family! Doing so would make us admit we have problems!

4. There is room for kindness and love, and even laughter, but watch out for that person's temper, or flash point. You'd best **walk on eggshells** if he or she is moody. Someone who lives with this person might silently cry, "Run!".

5. **Arrogance**, mixed with gossip and slander are common. Relationships outside the family are few. Non-blood persons must be fully in sync with the family's rules and value system to be accepted or tolerated.

6. Not often, but sometimes, alcoholism or some other addiction or **sin stronghold dominates** the family.

7. **"We never own blame.** If we did, that would mean we must take responsibility for our actions. Since others outside of family do not see eye to eye with us, they are obviously wrong and we are right! We will treat them as inferior and as outsiders." Many times in the carnal family there can be found examples of those who are controlled and abused and those who are controlling and abusive.

Remember: The arrogant, carnal {controlling} person never owns blame. The codependent {controlled} person takes the blame.

You see, the arrogant, carnal, controller might have to assume responsibility for her actions and attitudes if she owns up to wrong done. The codependent, controlled person feels he must assume responsibility for the controlling, abusive person. He feels that someone has to keep the peace so the tensions will subside. If others found out about this blame and punish cycle, they might, likewise blame him, the codependent one. Eventually the tension cools and the intense moody time period subsides. This sick, unhealthy relationship returns to a miserable dormant period until the next time the arrogant, carnal, controlling person blows another gasket. Then this sinful, destructive cycle starts all over again. There is no confession, no repentance, and no forgiveness, no emotional healing. By the way, if the codependent abused person ever stops "taking it", look out! Sparks will fly! Of course, this is exactly what needs to happen, hopefully with the help of a biblical counselor.

8. When something goes wrong **blame must be assigned** usually to a non-blood relative or non-family member. Other times the one blaming might target an immediate family member especially if he or she is weak and a good scapegoat. The powerful accusing person feels he is justified. What happens is that blame coupled with "behind closed doors" ridicule and sarcasm are meted out. Sometimes a secretive plan will emerge. The carnal family patria/matriarch will go to great lengths to punish, humiliate, and in worst cases, destroy the reputation and family ties of the person blamed. Woe to the family member that disagrees! If the scapegoat person is a mate or child, the sickening fear and sadness that is felt cannot be put into words. Four common, manipulative tactics these carnal, family power brokers use are:
    - **Accusation**
    - **Belittlement**
    - **Intimidation**
    - **Punishment**

9. Carnal family members remain offended for decades, **holding grudges**, remembering others sins, keeping records of wrongs, and possessing a general sense of insult, rejection, retribution and revenge. Once written off, you are written off for good.

10. **"What is best for the children will be best for the marriage."** The marriage in the carnal family, if intact, is the **lowest thing** on the priority list. Work, hobbies, children, and grandchildren all come before the marriage. There may be physical abuse and usually there is emotional abuse. Since the Lord Jesus is not allowed to rule according to His Word, the carnal marriage sinks to the bottom and gets only the leftovers. There may be an affair or two as well. Generational roots of addiction and private sin are usually deeply imbedded.

11. Various key people learn to **manipulate** other family members with "emotional hooks". Spoonfuls of guilt like this example are common: "So Tom, I understand that you, Peggy, and the kids are going to Peggy's parent's home for Christmas. Well that will be nice. …I guess your father and I will just sit home alone again on Christmas Eve… Say, did I tell you that the doctors are a bit concerned that your dad's stress levels are not helping his health? Oh well, you two and the grandkids…have a wonderful time."

12. Carnal families **require explanations** for decisions rather than simply respecting the person's decision at face value. This is big around the holidays in terms of who is and is not coming home for the big family dinner and festivities. In dealing with adult children there may be the following unspoken pressure, "Our gifts, and kindnesses toward you, son and your new wife, are directly related to your willingness

to cave in to our demands for information and reasons for your decisions. Now where are you spending Christmas?"

13. Rumors and big news travel at the **speed of light**. The rumor communication network is always kept in good working order. Usually one family member, say the middle or youngest sibling would be subconsciously given the role of **"Courier".** She takes it upon herself to act as family mediator or message carrier when trouble or conflict erupts within the extended family. Instead of family members talking directly with another family member to resolve conflict and reconcile, they end up using a "go between" which in this case is unhealthy.

14. If a carnal family were an old west **wagon wheel**, the controlling family member whether child or parent, will fight tooth and nail to maintain control of the central axle of the wagon wheel. Whoever wins and keeps the center axle position wields the power. In a biblical or Spirit-led family, all family members, especially dad and mom, insist that Jesus runs the show, that He is the center axle of the wheel. Even though dad is the family shepherd, head, protector, and servant-leader, and mom is the helpmate, nest maker, and main nurturer, they gladly submit themselves to the rule and authority of Jesus and His Word. Asking for forgiveness and quickly granting it are signs that Christ is the center of the home.

15. Sometimes there is performance-based **favoritism.** Example: Dad's favorite is the oldest daughter. Mom's her youngest son. It is also feasible that if there is a middle child, or one who bucks the carnal rules and family system, this poor kid might become the **scapegoat**. She is then often picked on, blamed at will for things out of her control, and, in general, rejected.

Remember this: **Favoritism produces hatred.** We see it clearly in Joseph's family in the Old Testament.

"Now Israel loved Joseph more than any of his other sons, because he had been born to him in his old age; and he made a richly ornamented robe for him. When his brothers saw that their father loved him more than any of them, they hated him and could not speak a kind word to him." (Genesis 37:3, 4)

Consequences for Breaking the Family Rules

Simply put, if you are blood family, you will be forgiven most likely. If you are non-blood family, as in a daughter or son in-law or simply not related at all, there is almost no chance of ever being forgiven. You may be tolerated but never fully embraced as family. Breaking small rules might be overlooked with some scorn, shame, and subtle chastisement and rejection.

Breaking big rules means unfortunately that chances of **being forgiven** and **fully reinstated** to blood family are almost nonexistent.

The cost is high when you decide to follow Christ because in so doing, you are also breaking the carnal family's rules. Since God has forgiven us, Barbara and I have chosen to forgive people from the past with no strings attached. We no longer choose to blame any of the people that hurt and betrayed us. That is what Christ did for us. Jesus was crucified. He forgave His crucifiers. We must also forgive.

Luke 23:34 says:

Jesus said, "Father, forgive them, for they do not know what they are doing."

Small Group Discussion — Chapter 6

1. Of the 15 carnal family rules mentioned in this chapter, which three rules have touched your life or relationships?

   _______ _______ _______

   Please go back through the chapter and circle these numbers for easy reference. Please share why you chose the ones you did.

2. What would life be like if a teenager in the carnal family decides to surrender her life to Christ and His Word and begins to live out her Spirit-directed faith at home?

3. What would life be like if one marriage partner decided to no longer obey these carnal rules and the other partner insisted they be followed?

4. If possible, have each couple go off to be alone together to ask each other the following **Bridge Builder** question. Let your partner share while you listen attentively. When they are done, say to them the **Four Magic Words: "Please tell me more"**, and then listen lovingly again. Don't fix, don't correct, and don't disagree. Just listen attentively. Prize them. If time permits, summarize back to your partner what you believe you heard them say. In doing this, you demonstrate that you listened and that you value them. Then reverse roles and repeat the listening and sharing process.

Here is your fourth **Bridge Builder** question:

If there is one thing that I do—a priority that I uphold, or an attitude I express—for which you are thankful or proud, what is it?

5. Please ask for prayer requests and then close in prayer.

Chapter 7

Our Anchor

If two rowboats meant to be together in the middle of the lake are to stay there, they must be anchored well. Your Anchor is the Lord Jesus Christ and His Word.

He, who saves your soul, keeps your marriage.

Without Him you will drift, sink, and be lost.

As you walk by faith in this Christian life, you must also remain married by faith. If you are depending on anything other than the Lord Jesus to sustain you or your relationships, you will finish this life poorly and will regret the way you lived.

Anchoring your marriage to Christ means you agree it is not "your" marriage, but God's. Matthew 19:4-6 reads:

"'Haven't you read,' he replied, 'that at the beginning the Creator made them male and female,' and said, 'For this reason a man will leave his father and mother and be united to his wife, and the two will become one flesh'? So they are no longer two, but one. ***Therefore what God has joined together****, let man not separate.'"* (Bold added)

In the King James Version, the word for "separate" is translated "put asunder" which in the Greek means, "to place room between, that is, part; reflexively to go away: —depart, put asunder, separate." (Strong's Exhaustive Concordance)

Malachi 2:15,16 reads:

"Has not the LORD made them one? In flesh and spirit they are his. And why one? Because he was seeking godly offspring. So guard yourself in your spirit, and do not break faith with the wife of your youth.

"I hate divorce," *says the LORD God of Israel, "and I hate a man's covering himself with violence as well as with his garment," says the LORD Almighty. So guard yourself in your spirit, and do not break faith."* (Bold added)

You see you do not have the authority or the right to tamper with or tarnish anything God has ordained. Since your God hates divorce, you must hate divorce. Why would you ever do anything that God hates? If you belong to God, then you and everything you hold dear must be in subjection to His will, His desires, His plan, and according to His Word, the Bible.

Have you, once and for all, settled the questions—Do you belong to God? Are you going to Heaven? Are you a child of God? Is Jesus Christ really your personal Lord, Savior, and Master? Who is your anchor in life? When all else fails you, will your anchor also fail you? When others betray and lie to you, will your anchor do likewise? Consider the following questions in light of what the Bible says:

1. **Where did you come from?**

    - God loves you and created you to know Him personally. He is loving and true and would never lie to you.

      "*For God so loved the world that he gave his one and only Son, that whoever believes in him shall not perish but have eternal life*". (John 3:16)

      "Now this is eternal life: that they may know you, the only true God, and Jesus Christ, whom you have sent." (John 17:3)

    - The One True God of the Bible who loves you, formed you in your mother's womb.

      "For you created my inmost being; you knit me together in my mother's womb. I praise you because I am fearfully and wonderfully made; your works are wonderful, I know that full well." (Psalm 139:13, 14)

2. **If God has created you and loves you, what is preventing you from knowing Him intimately?**

    God wants to give you a fresh start. A clean slate is just a prayer away.

    - You are sinful and separated from God, so you cannot know Him intimately or experience His saving, keeping, and protecting love.

      "For all have sinned and fall short of the glory of God," (Romans 3:23)

"For the wages of sin is death, but the gift of God is eternal life in Christ Jesus our Lord." (Romans 6:23)

- Just as fire and gasoline cannot be together, those who have the stain of sin can never be in the presence of a holy, sinless, and perfect God.

  "our God is holy." (Psalm 99:9b)

  "the stain of your guilt is still before me," (Jeremiah 2:22b)

- You must be pardoned. Your sin must be forever washed away.

- God created man to have fellowship with Him, but due to his own stubborn self-will, he chose to go his own independent, selfish way, and fellowship was broken. This self-will, characterized by an attitude of active rebellion or passive indifference, is an evidence of what the Bible calls sin.

God is holy and man is sinful. A great gulf separates the two. The arrows illustrate that man is continually trying to reach God and establish a personal relationship with Him through his own efforts, such as a good life, philosophy, or religion—but he inevitably fails.

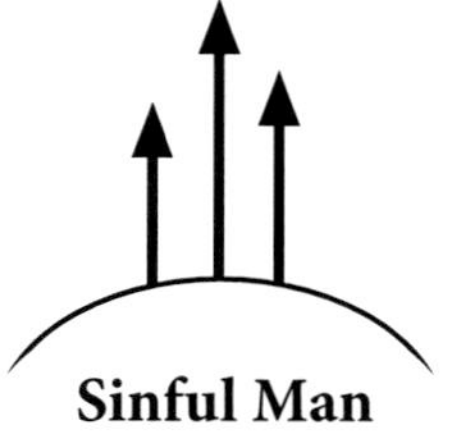

3. **If there were only ONE WAY to bridge this gulf, would you want to know it?**

   In 1830, George Wilson was tried by the U.S. court in Philadelphia for robbery and murder and was sentenced to hang. Andrew Jackson, President of the United States, granted him a presidential pardon. But Wilson refused the pardon, insisting it was not a pardon unless he accepted it. The question was brought before the U. S. Supreme Court, and Chief Justice John Marshall wrote the following decision: "A pardon is a paper, the value of which depends upon its acceptance by the person implicated. It's hardly to be supposed that one under sentence of death would refuse to accept a pardon, but if it is refused, it is no pardon. George Wilson must hang." What was the outcome? George Wilson was hanged.[1]

- Jesus Christ is God's **only** provision for man's sin. Through Him alone we can know God intimately, be fully pardoned for our sin, and experience His unconditional love.

  "*Salvation is found in no one else, for there is no other name under heaven given to men by which we must be saved.*" (Acts 4:12)

- He died in our place and rose from the dead.

  "*But God demonstrates his own love for us in this: While we were still sinners, Christ died for us.*" (Romans 5:8)

"Christ died for our sins...He was buried...He was raised on the third day according to the Scriptures. He appeared to Peter, then to the twelve. After that He appeared to more than five hundred." (1 Corinthians 15:3-6)

- He is the only way to God.

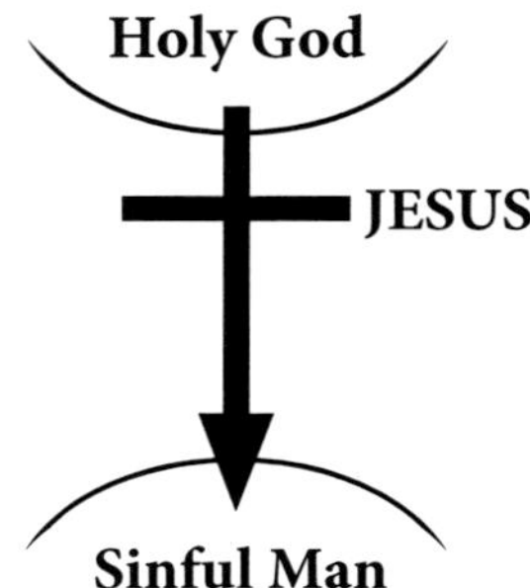

This diagram illustrates that God has bridged the gulf that separates us from Him by sending His Son, Jesus Christ. He chose to die on the cross in our place to pay the penalty for our sins.

- Those who love darkness, reject Christ, and refuse His free offer of forgiveness and new life will perish. They will be eternally condemned for their sins. The wrath of God will fall on them.

"They perish because they refused to love the truth and so be saved. For this reason God sends them a powerful delusion so that they will believe the lie and so that all will be condemned who have not believed the truth but have delighted in wickedness." (2 Thessalonians 7: 10b-12)

4. **What must occur in order for you to be saved from your sins and eternal death and be assured of complete forgiveness and Heaven?**

    - You must individually receive Jesus Christ as Savior and Lord. Then you can know God personally and experience His love.

    - You must receive Christ. {Gladly welcome Him}

      "Yet to all who received him, to those who believed in his name, he gave the right to become children of God." (John 1:12)

    - You receive Christ by faith.

      "For it is by grace you have been saved, through faith—and this not from yourselves, it is the gift of God—not by works, so that no one can boast." (Ephesians 2:8,9)

      If someone were to say, "I hope to get to heaven because I'm a pretty good person". "I'm hoping the good outweighs the bad". How would you respond to this person?

    - When you receive Christ, you experience a New Birth. {Read John 3:1-8 if time permits}

    - You receive Christ by personal invitation.

      [Christ speaking]
      "Behold, I stand at the door and knock. If anyone hears My voice and opens the door, I will come in..." (Revelation 3:20 NKJV)

Receiving Christ involves turning to God from sin and self-rule (repentance) and trusting Christ to come into our lives to forgive us of our sins and to make us what He wants us to be. Just to agree intellectually that Jesus Christ is the Son of God is not enough. Nor is it enough to have an emotional experience. We receive Christ by faith, as an act of our will.

- When you receive Christ, a Great Exchange occurs instantly!

  First: Jesus takes all of your past, present, and future sin, condemnation, and guilt away. Back on that Cross, Jesus removed your sins and placed them on Himself. He was crucified, became guilty on your behalf, and was condemned. He then suffered torment in Hell so you would not have to. He freed you from the penalty and power of sin.

  Second: In exchange, Jesus gives you His righteousness and His life. You are forgiven, unable to be condemned, holy, blameless, pure, and forever innocent of all charges. You have eternal life. God, the Father, now sees you holy and perfect. He loves you the same as He loves Jesus. This exchange is irrevocable. It is finished!

  "I delight greatly in the LORD; my soul rejoices in my God. For he has clothed me with garments of salvation and arrayed me in a robe of righteousness, as a bridegroom adorns his head like a priest and as a bride adorns herself with her jewels." (Isaiah 61:10)

5. **Would you like to receive Christ right now by faith through prayer?**

The following is a suggested prayer:

Lord Jesus, I need You. I want to be assured of going to Heaven when I die. I also want to know You personally. Thank you for dying on the cross for my sins. I open the door of my life and receive You as my Savior and Lord.

Thank You for forgiving me of my sins and giving me eternal life. Take control of the throne of my life. Make me the kind of person You want me to be.

- Remember: Jesus is now in your life. You belong to Him. He will never leave you nor forsake you. You are God's own son or daughter. The Bible promises eternal life to all who receive Christ.

Heaven is your new home!

"And this is the testimony: God has given us eternal life, and this life is in his Son. He who has the Son has life; he who does not have the Son of God does not have life. I write these things to you who believe in the name of the Son of God so that you may know that you have eternal life." (1 John 5:11-13)

"My sheep listen to my voice; I know them, and they follow me. I give them eternal life, and they shall never perish; no one can snatch them out of my hand. My Father, who has given them to me, is greater than all; no one can snatch them out of my Father's hand." (John 10:27-29)

What comfort and assurance is God giving you right now?

1. **Please read the following verses out loud.**

   "*All that the Father gives me will come to me, and whoever comes to me I will never drive away. For I have come down from heaven not to do my will but to do the will of him who sent me. And this is the will of him who sent me, that I shall lose none of all that he has given me, but raise them up at the last day.*" (John 6:37-39)

   "*For I am convinced that neither death nor life, neither angels nor demons, neither the present nor the future, nor any powers, neither height nor depth, nor anything else in all creation, will be able to separate us from the love of God that is in Christ Jesus our Lord.*" (Romans 8:38,39

   What doubts might you still have concerning your assurance of your salvation and your eternal security?

   If you were to die tonight, how assured are you of going straight to Heaven?

   0%———25%———50%———75%———100%

2. **Work on memorizing the following definition of Faith. This is the same definition discussed in other chapters of this book. Then discuss it and apply this faith principle to your assurance of being forgiven and going to Heaven someday.**

"Faith is choosing to live as though the Bible is true, regardless of circumstances, emotions, or cultural trends."

---

[1]Life Builders. Destined for Security. Campus Crusade for Christ, 2003: pp. 13-14.

Small Group Discussion — Chapter 7

1. If you were a rowboat in the middle of a big lake and you had no anchor, what would happen to you over time?

2. In terms of where you will spend eternity, what will happen to you if you are not anchored to the Lord Jesus Christ?

3. Why do you think that a majority of Christians (roughly 51%, Barna Research) feels that at some point in the future, God will change His mind about them and reject them?

4. Ask some members of the small group to voluntarily share when and how they chose to trust Jesus Christ as their own personal Lord, Savior, King, and Master of their life and eternal destiny. (Note: You may wish to enlist certain group members to do this the week prior to gathering so they will have time to prepare their personal journey with God.

5. If possible, have each couple go off to be alone together to ask each other the following **Bridge Builder** question. Let your partner share while you listen attentively. When they are done, say to them the **Four Magic Words: "Please tell me more"**, and then listen lovingly again. Don't fix, don't correct, and don't disagree. Just listen attentively. Prize them. If time permits, summarize back to your partner what you believe you heard them say. In doing this, you demonstrate

that you listened and that you value them. Then reverse roles and repeat the listening and sharing process.

Here is your fifth **Bridge Builder** question:

What is your greatest wish, dream, or hope?

6. Please ask for prayer requests and then close in prayer.

Chapter 8

Seven Ropes to Tie Two Boats

If you recall, in the first chapter we talked about Green Lake, Wisconsin and its quiet beauty on a warm August evening. Remember the idea of drifting was brought up. Two rowboats that are meant to be together will eventually drift apart due to the natural forces of the lake and nature.

In addition to the essential requirement of the Lord Jesus being the faithful, strong Anchor of your marriage, Barbara and I want to get real practical with you. Couples that come in for biblical counseling have none of the following seven ropes tying their two rowboats together. To keep from drifting, you need the seven ropes that will tie your two rowboats tightly together. Couples with teachable and humble hearts that tie their marriage with these seven ropes do not break up. They have disciplined themselves in obedient surrender to the Lord Jesus Christ. They have chosen to hold fast together and let nothing get in between them. Nothing!

First Rope—*Hold Hands Everywhere*

Some people think this concept is shallow and silly. It does not matter what they think. It works! We teach couples to hold hands when walking, shopping, and sitting in church, even attending funerals! Remember God has called you and your mate to be as one. Show it. Some folks give Barbara and me a second glance at the grocery store. We keep reminding ourselves that not only is this good for our marriage but on lookers might catch the contagion as well. We are learning that leadership is modeling and modeling is everything. A few years ago, Barbara and I were near the front row participating in our church's worship service. We almost always hold hands and when some of our children would sit with us, we made sure that Barbara and I were together, side by side.

This particular Sunday after the service was over, a young teenage girl about 16 came over to us and said something that quite honestly we did not expect. "You don't know me," she said, "but I have been watching you two from a distance for many weeks now. I hardly know anything about you except for one thing: Someday when I have a husband, I want a marriage just like yours!" Barbara and I were both humbled and grateful to God that He had burdened our hearts to hold hands and hold fast our love for God and, thus, for each other.

When you hold hands, you are telling the world:

- You are in love.
- God was right in bringing you two together.
- You are fulfilling God's plan by filling each other's gaps (hands clasped together). You need each other's strengths and weaknesses.

- You want to honor God by your commitment to each other.

Ecclesiastes 4:9,10 reads, " *Two are better than one, because they have a good return for their work: If one falls down, his friend can help him up. But pity the man who falls and has no one to help him up!*"

Just remember two hands together are better than two hands apart!

Second Rope—*Same Bed Time*

One of the questions we ask couples the first or second counseling visit is, "Do you both go to bed together at the same time?" One mate for a host of reasons is usually dead exhausted at 8:00 PM. They have been with takers all day long and their adrenaline reserves are utterly depleted. The other mate tends to look forward to the later hours. Perhaps he is a night owl, likes to unwind in front of the TV with his remote securely in his hand.

We have found that married couples care for each other better and are less likely to get involved in sin via the movie channels or the Internet when they go to bed together. We have also found that nothing good happens after midnight. With the average person needing somewhere between 7 and 8 hours of sleep per night, going to bed together at a reasonable agreed upon hour works best. If one wants to sleep right away but the other needs to unwind, make use of such things as earplugs, sleep eye masks, and small, clip on reading lights. Remember if the devil has a middle name it would probably be "Isolation". Going to bed together at the same time promotes oneness, togetherness, and marital love.

Third Rope—*Cuddle Pray at Bedtime*

Couples that sincerely pray to the Lord out loud together on a daily basis remain strong in their love for God and each other and they finish well in life. Our experience has shown that about 95% of Christian couples do not pray together out loud on a regular basis. It is good to pray out loud together during meals at home and at restaurants. It is also wonderful to pray with your children at bedtime.

The kind of praying that we see so desperately lacking in Christian marriages is where the husband and wife privately pray together out loud on a daily basis away from the dinner table, perhaps in their own bedroom, in the car, or while taking a walk outside.

In Christian marriage, the most important level of intimacy is your prayer life with God and your mate. Barbara and I model and teach bedtime cuddle praying. We start out in the middle of our queen-sized bed. We spend 5, maybe 10 minutes there. I wrap my arms around my lovely wife, Barbara, and then I pray a short prayer to the Lord out loud something like, *"Lord, thanks for this day and your blessings. Please watch over us, our home, and our kids and their homes. Thanks for Barbara and please bless her tonight."*

Barbara then prays out loud something like, *"Well Lord, please give us good rest, we're beat. Help us to shine your truth and love to each other, our family, and to everyone. Watch over Jim and his doctor's appointment tomorrow. Please also encourage Mike and Carol since Mike just lost his job".* Some nights the prayers are much shorter if we are both exhausted. After this short prayer, and a few minutes of just holding one another, I roll over on my left side and she usually holds me. Eventually we separate to our respective sides of the bed. We have missed a few nights and sometimes only one person prays. Ninety percent of the time, we both pray out loud in cuddle praying.

Intimacy in marriage is like the three interdependent layers of rain forest foliage. Imagine for a moment you are in one of the lushest rain forests in existence. In studying the various layers of forest foliage, you discover three canopies of plant life. You will commonly find the tall **avocado** trees providing cover at the top, **essential** in distributing rain and sunlight to the lower two levels. At the middle level you might find the shorter **banana** trees designed by God to provide the right covering for the lowest level. On the floor of this amazingly fertile place, you can find coffee plants growing providing rich **coffee** beans.

The three levels of rain forest are unique and interdependent. If the top canopy is destroyed, the remaining ecosystem will be severely stressed and much life will perish. The pounding sunlight will destroy the middle and lower levels. The direct, torrential rains would also cause massive erosion and much of this beautiful habitat would be lost.

Often if there is a deficiency or problem at the ground level, then just look up, way up. The reason for the ground problem may very well be found by studying the top level.

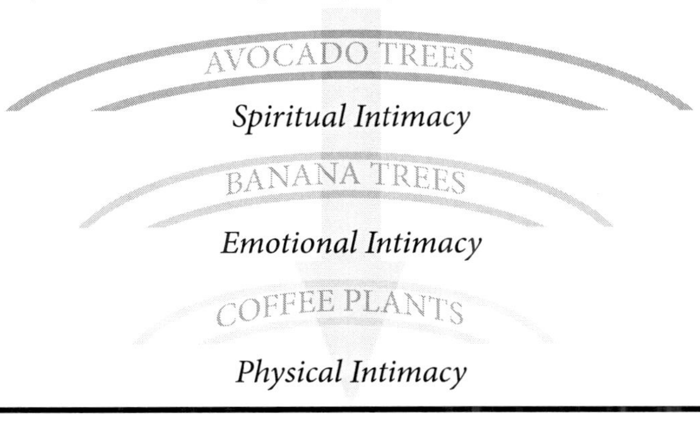

AVOCADO TREES

Spiritual Intimacy

BANANA TREES

Emotional Intimacy

COFFEE PLANTS

Physical Intimacy

Intimacy in marriage
has everything to do with prayer.

The highest level of intimacy established in marriage is "spiritual intimacy". This is why Satan attacks first and foremost at this level. He knows that if a Christian married couple prays out loud together, much of his wicked efforts will fail. He and his demons especially hate it and tremble when you pray **out loud.** He cannot read your mind but he has to listen to your voice. If you are drifting from your Lord, you will find it difficult to pray out loud with your mate.

Ephesians 4:26,27: reads, *"'In your anger do not sin': Do not let the sun go down while you are still angry, and do not give the devil a foothold."* If you go to bed angry, he won't have to hear you two praying out loud to the King of Kings and Lord of Lords, the Lord Jesus. If this does not happen, then while you slumber, the devil, will be establishing strongholds of wickedness. Then he will move in to further isolate you two.

The next or middle level of marital intimacy is "emotional intimacy". If you are humble and honest before God, possessing a clean, forgiving heart, God will begin to bless your emotional relationship with you and your mate. One rule Barbara and I live by is the **Ten Minute Tiff Rule.** When you have a spat or heated disagreement, agree with God as your witness to come together and resolve the tiff and forgive or ask forgiveness within 10 minutes. Sometimes you need a little time to cool down, collect yourself, and experience the gentle nudge of your loving Heavenly Father. Ten minutes is plenty of time to deal with it and get over it.

Remember, you are on the same team! Some couples have never resolved or reconciled their tiffs. We met with one wife recently who slept in a separate room for a week because she and her husband were still stewing in the juices of grudge holding, resentment, and unforgiveness. It is time to choose to no longer be offended!

Ephesians 4:29-32 reads, "*Do not let any unwholesome talk come out of your mouths, but only what is helpful for building others up according to their needs, that it may benefit those who listen. And do not grieve the Holy Spirit of God, with whom you were sealed for the day of redemption. Get rid of all bitterness, rage and anger, brawling and slander, along with every form of malice. Be kind and compassionate to one another, forgiving each other, just as in Christ God forgave you.*"

The final level of marital intimacy is "physical intimacy". When you and your mate unconditionally give yourself to one another and bless one another in this way, God is pleased and glorified. Barbara and I spend almost no counseling time on sexual intimacy. Why? It is because sexual intimacy is just like the ground level of the rain forest. When you address the problems in the top and middle levels, the ground level issues become resolved.

As you bless one another during intimacy, your act is a testimony of how good God is to you. Your sexual intimacy is a way of saying "Thank you" to God. As a couple, frequently, act out your gratefulness to God.

Fourth Rope—*Insist on the Weekly Date*

This Rope is plain and simple. Always plan and have your weekly date. Barbara and I, on Fridays, will often schedule in a lunch at Moy's Chinese restaurant in Elkhorn. We take a good hour and sometimes an hour and a half to eat, relax, and unwind from the intense pressures of counseling and ministry. We always hold hands. We laugh and chat with the wait staff.

We guard this time. Only required trips, illness, or emergencies will keep us from our special time together. If Friday is a wash, then we pick Thursday or even Saturday morning to go out and get some good, hot coffee, bacon, eggs, hash browns, and toast or biscuits. Stop drooling and make plans. If you do not make such plans and guard them, the urgency of other good activities and demands will rob you. In time, you will drift apart.

If nothing is planned, well, guess what results?

We met one struggling couple with 5 children. During 17 years of marriage since their brief honeymoon, they had not scheduled any sort of over night get away for just the two of them. They were good people and wonderful parents, but they were toast! They were exhausted and snipping at one another. You see, because of their love for their kids, they became what we call the "Parent-Centered Marriage". We train couples to be "Marriage-Centered Parents".

What often happens over the years, while Mom pours her life into her beloved children, Dad gets caught up in his work and hobbies. The job and the kids get most of the attention, but the marriage slowly dissolves. When the kids all finally leave the nest, mom and dad look at each other as strangers. Divorce often results. You must decide upon a stubborn unyielding resolve to become Marriage-Centered. You will get flak for it. Take it like good soldiers. God will be very pleased and He will bless you down the road. If you do not cultivate and tend to your marriage like good gardeners, weeds of isolation, disinterest, and affairs usually result.

Fifth Rope—*Return Blessings*

Nothing is more repulsive to one's flesh then to show kindness and favor toward someone who has hurt or betrayed you. This fifth rope is just as difficult as the third rope: Cuddle Praying. Many movies have the theme of revenge. Payback is a central theme in most cultures. Unfortunately it is also a favorite pastime in marriage.

God's Word is quite clear. Read what the Apostle Peter wrote:

"Finally, all of you, live in harmony with one another; be sympathetic, love as brothers, be compassionate and humble. Do not repay evil with evil or insult with insult, but with blessing, because to this you were called so that you may inherit a blessing." (I Peter 3:8,9)

Note the following:

- You were called or commanded to return blessings. God has ordered you!

- He wants you to inherit blessings, not curses. Disobedience brings curses. Obedience brings blessings. It is your choice. What do you want?

Some mates return insults immediately with yelling, door slamming, throwing things, name calling, and even hitting which is illegal and a criminal offense. Immediate insults also include giving the "silent treatment" or taking off to go to a bar or on a spending spree.

Other mates return insults in a quiet, delayed manner. They will appear forgiving, yet a week, or even a month later, they might inflict their strike when least expected. "Honey, I am sorry that you will need to cancel your hunting trip, but I am just not feeling very well…" Nice effect! It always boils down to this:

Will you obey God or your flesh?

Let us say your husband comes home exhausted and preoccupied with struggles at work. He more or less ignores you (you take this as an insult), and he plops down in front of the T.V.. You could say to yourself, "Well, bucko, two can play this game!" or you can obey God and receive a blessing later by doing a quiet, loving, and an undeserved act of kindness. This might look like, "Honey, I bet your day was draining and difficult. Here is your favorite soda and some chips. Sit up a bit and I will rub your shoulders to help you relax." Now don't let your motive be to get a blessing back from him. Rather seek only to please God. Remember, He promises you will inherit a blessing from Him.

Learn to bless your mate. Show grace and mercy to your mate. Remember that grace is giving to someone that which he or she does not deserve and mercy is withholding that which he or she does deserve. As Jesus did toward the young woman caught in adultery, give what is needed, not what is deserved.

Say you have a nice boat that you are securing in the water to a sturdy pier. If you only tie one end of the boat to the pier with rope, the other end will probably be tossed around by the wind and waves. It is always best to tie both ends of the boat securely with good rope.

Here is a quick exercise:

Place your mate directly in front of you. Now apart from Jesus, you know what he deserves! But you, by a choice of the will, bless him with your **left hand on his right shoulder.** Think of this as issuing the same grace that God issues to you. You are going to give to him that which he does not deserve and can never earn such as affirmation, kindness, forgiveness, and support.

Now, similar to properly securing the boat with two ropes to the pier, you further bless him by placing your **right hand on his left shoulder.** Think of this as issuing the same mercy that God issues to you. By a sacrificial act of your will (faith), choose to withhold from him that which he does deserve apart from Christ such as rejection, criticism, or a cold shoulder.

Do now what comes natural. Use both arms and slowly pull him close and hold him safe and secure. Tell him how much you love him. After doing this, simply reverse roles and have the husband or fiancé initiate the **"blessing ropes"** of grace and mercy. This shows how God loves you and how you must love each other.

Remember the miseries discussed in Chapter 6, The Rules of The Carnal Family? The worst thing a couple can do is leave conflicts unresolved. Decide right now that no sun will ever set on your unresolved conflicts and anger. We recommend a three step approach in dealing with your conflicts. As soon as God convicts you (gets through your tough hide of pride), do three things:

- **Pursue** the offended person.
- **Admit** your failure.
- **Request** their forgiveness.

The sweetest, yet rare occurrence is when both of you meet each other mid way in the hall as a result of God's conviction upon your own heart. Wow! That would be cool! If both your hearts are soft toward God and each other, God will reinstate intimacy.

Sixth Rope—*Establish Talk Times*

It is vital to establish regular, disciplined talk times. For some couples, once a week will do. Others need a sharing debriefing time every day. One couple lights a candle and takes the phone off the hook for 10 minutes every eve when both get home from their daily activities. Others go for walks or lunch or breakfast dates. These talk times like the weekly date must be guarded jealously and insisted upon.

One older couple that had 12 children knew they would not survive without close, loving, honest, and supportive communication. Each evening when both returned from their jobs, they would light a candle and place it on the kitchen table. The kids playing rambunctiously in the background knew that this was "Mom and Dad's Time" and they had better respect it. This husband and wife just took turns sharing their **High Point** and then their **Low Point** of the day respectively. While the one was sharing, the other just listened and comforted and affirmed. They did not try to fix one another or correct one another. They just loved through quiet, tender listening.

During one of these daily talk times, a couple of the kids upstairs started yelling and making all kinds of racket. Mother stopped the talk time session for just a second and she called out to them, "Is there any blood?" There was no answer, so she and her husband continued their talk time. After all, this was "their" time!

Suggested Talk Time Questions and Ideas

Remember to listen more, and talk less.
God gave you two ears and one mouth.

1. Thinking back, what was the most uplifting, memorable time of our marriage?

2. When do you feel loved, valued, or respected by me the most?

3. What has been the most treasured gift that I have given you and why?

4. If there is one thing that I do, a priority that I uphold, or an attitude I express for which you are thankful or proud, what is it?

5. What is your greatest wish, dream, or hope?

6. What is your deepest fear or worry?

7. Please share with me your greatest need right now.

8. What, could I do to be more considerate so that you would feel more loved, valued or listened to?

9. What area of my life do you see as needing work?

10. What is one thing you'd want God to do for our relationship?

11. Share one thing that is draining, bothering, frustrating, or discouraging you.

12. Share one thing that is bringing you hope, fulfillment, and joy.

13. Share one thing that you are wishing for, dreaming for, or praying for.
14. What was the most discouraging thing (low point) about your day?
15. What was the most encouraging thing (high point) about your day?

Seventh Rope—*Serve in Church Together*

Remember, if God has you married, then He intends to shine His truth and love to others through the oneness and togetherness of your marriage. Barbara and I encourage you, if possible, to not just go to church together, but also to serve together. We know in some cases this will be difficult but we find it a great way to be together and to be a witness as a team. We recommend you serve God together just like you should take vacations together and sleep in the same bed together.

We are all for some time away from each other like ladies night out or the men going golfing. What is frustrating to us is to see a tired married couple barely getting any quality time together all week and then we separate them even further when they get to church.

If possible, we urge you to serve as a team. If I am asked to teach a class, Barbara will be there in the front row praying for me and encouraging me onward. I will have her speak now and then as well. Later on in the year, if the church asks her to teach the Kindergarten class, she will teach and I will be her assistant.

We know there are exceptions but we believe you should strive to serve together. This way you grow in love and strength being with each other and others will see Christ's love and kindness in your united service. We trust that God will bless you as you implement these ropes into your marriage.

1. Why do tying two rowboats together on the lake keep them from drifting apart? How can this apply to your marriage?

2. Of the following **seven** ropes to tie **two** boats together, please circle two that are the most helpful for you as a couple. Put a check √ in the box by the **one** rope that is or might be the most challenging for you to tie. Then if you'd like to, share why?

   ☐ Hold Hands Everywhere

   ☐ Same Bed Time

   ☐ Cuddle Pray at Bedtime

   ☐ Insist on the Weekly Date

   ☐ Return Blessings

   ☐ Establish Talk Times

   ☐ Serve in Church Together

3. If possible, have each couple go off to be alone together to ask each other the following **Bridge Builder** question. Let your partner share while you listen attentively. When they are done, say to them the **Four Magic Words: "Please tell me more"**, and then listen lovingly again. Don't fix, don't correct, and don't disagree. Just listen attentively. Prize them. If time permits, summarize back to your partner what you

believe you heard them say. In doing this, you demonstrate that you listened and that you value them. Then reverse roles and repeat the listening and sharing process.

Here is your sixth **Bridge Builder** question:

What is your deepest fear or worry?

4. Facilitator—remind the group to have read all of the **Wave Makers and Wave Calmers so as to complete their "Growth Assignment"** (page 142). They will be discussed next week "Couple To Couple".

5. Please ask for prayer requests and then close in prayer.

Chapter 9

Symptoms of the Suffering Family

During my high school years, long before meeting Jim, I spent wonderful summers with my family at our lake home on Powers Lake in Wisconsin. Those were years filled with fond, warm memories. I felt safe most of the time.

One summer day when I was sixteen, I decided to take our 2-person Butterfly Sailboat out. The sky was blue and the sun provided warmth. As I sailed by myself, I remember how wonderful I felt as the gentle breeze filled my sail and soothed my skin.

I reached the center of the lake late that afternoon. As I attempted to turn about and head back, I lost control of the sail and my boat began to tip. I frantically tried to stabilize her but to no avail. In a matter of seconds, my sailboat tipped over and turned completely upside down with the sail and mast pointing downward under the water.

Although I had my life jacket on, I froze with fear. I was all alone and a mile from the shore. I was not confident enough to attempt to swim the distance and I was afraid to just leave the capsized boat out in the middle of nowhere. I thought, "What if no one sees me? What will I do if it starts to get dark?" I should not have forged ahead being such a novice.

I waited for what seemed the longest time. In reality, it was probably around 30 minutes before a guy in a boat came by close enough to see my frantically waving hands and overturned boat. I remember the great feeling I had in being discovered. I was thankful not to have to face my predicament alone.

Earlier I had tried to flip the sail boat upright but was neither strong enough nor had enough weight to matter. I guess that is one of the reasons why they call it a 2-person sailboat. Two people are required to return the boat easily to its proper, upright position. This kind man actually had to jump from his boat into the water to help me. After explaining what both of us had to do, and trying numerous times, together, exerting much force and expending all my remaining energy, the boat flipped back to its correct, upright position.

I thanked him profusely and although totally exhausted, I slowly made it back to our pier. I learned a good lesson that day: Don't go out on the water alone! I experienced fear and great fatigue but in terms of real suffering, I did not even scratch the surface.

Most of us when we are young know little about suffering. Life can be a stern and demanding teacher as it has been for people throughout history. At age 16, I did not have a clue.

Different Kinds Of Suffering

Jim and I are convinced now that nothing hurts worse than a broken heart. Your dreams are dashed, a loved one dies, you get sick, family and friends betray or ignore you, your prayers seem to go unanswered year upon year, someone you trust abuses you; just a few heart breakers.

We want to share with you some of the symptoms of suffering that we and many other families have experienced when the brutality of life hits with gale force winds. Whether dealing with long-term illness, divorce, untimely death, abortion, miscarriages, financial difficulties, or many other challenges, the following symptoms are quite commonly experienced.

Historian Roy Nichols (1896-1972) writes,

"The most beautiful people I have known are those who have known defeat, known suffering, known struggle, known loss, and have found their way out of the depths.

These people have an appreciation, sensitivity, and an understanding of life that fills them with compassion, gentleness, and a deep loving concern. Beautiful people do not just happen."

Families that are suffering for various reasons may relate to the following:

1. You feel intense **helplessness** with periods of depressing **numbness**.

2. You have **less vitality** than before. You have "fewer energy bullets." Remember that if God only gives you 3 energy bullets today, only spend 3 energy bullets. Do not feel

you must squeeze out a 4th or 5th bullet to please people or church.

3. If you are battling a long term illness or disability, you may experience tremendous **guilt** because you feel like you are letting everyone down. You may feel like you are a burden to the family and a drain to your church.

4. The other family members who are the care givers to the "sick one" experience **real pain** too.

    - If in this category, you may experience **survivor guilt**. Simply put, you are not the one suffering. Why not you?

    - You are frustrated because you cannot **fix**, rescue, or heal your loved one.

    - You may taste anger because your family is no longer **normal**.

5. If there is suffering and pain at home, you are tired of trying to **measure up** at church, in the community, at work, and even maybe with some relatives who don't get it.

Now take a moment before reading further and quietly pause in silence. Please meditate on the following two verses. Let God speak to your heart.

"I want to know Christ and the power of his resurrection and the fellowship of sharing in his sufferings, becoming like him in his death," (Philippians 3:10)

"But those who suffer he delivers in their suffering; he speaks to them in their affliction." (Job 36:15)

If you find yourself relating to some of these symptoms, you are quite human and normal unless you are protecting your wounded heart with denial. If any of the above resonates with you, just tell your Lord about it. Tell Him everything. Don't withhold anything. Crawl into His big lap and give Him the things that pain you. He can handle it!

"Trust in him at all times, O people; pour out your hearts to him, for God is our refuge." (Psalm 62:8)

No matter what struggle you are going through, two things will be true. First is that pain is pain. It does no good to compare your pain or loss with that of another. Second, your Heavenly Father understands your pain and suffering and He will not only comfort you but He will get you through it.

If you are in a suffering family, you may be experiencing at least 5 more symptoms:

6. You dread collapsing or **caving in** from the constant heaviness and seriousness of it all. There can be a great **loss of dignity**. Damage from a stroke, hair loss from chemo, financial mismanagement, or suffering a divorce are only a few battles that can rob dignity. Some people either avoid you or marginalize you: "Oh, you're divorced." "So you are the one who failed." "I understand you have the *disease*…cancer!"

7. You may experience **relentless suspense** concerning the final outcome of whatever is causing the suffering. You may fear collection agencies, or the next blood test, biopsy, or court date. Perhaps your mate has left you for another and you don't know if he is coming back. Even if he did, what would that mean? The misery and suspense are real.

You may have suffered terrible loss with either miscarriages or the loss of a child or loved one. The pain is intense and no one can understand unless they have gone through it. You may actually **personify** the source of all the suffering and pain. You allow yourself to be emotionally tortured, flogged, and taunted by its sadistic, condemning, mocking **presence**. It just never seems to go away. You may feel like you have failed or that you are a marked person or couple. This tension seems to define you.

For example, living with cancer becomes almost unbearable. It is like living with a cruel, Nazi torturer playing Russian roulette with your family. He teases, torments, and instills dread. "*Will I take her life now or will I wait a few months or years? Hmmm. Let's see.*"

8. You may develop a **simmering anger**. Like a slow, burning pile of leaves in autumn, you smolder. You begin to take your anger out on family, pets, co-workers, soda/snack machines, electronic equipment, etc. Tensions build amongst family members, particularly between husband and wife. A distancing or **isolation** settles in like a quiet, yet noticeable fog. Children **quarrel**. They begin to tilt from stress overload. Disrespect increases. Grades and behaviors may fluctuate. They may not have the emotional hardware to deal with it.

9. You may develop **Post Traumatic Stress** symptoms. Physical, emotional, or medical problems seem to surface such as:

Migraine headaches	Depression
Panic attacks	Tightening of the chest

Neck, back, shoulder pain	Heart palpitations
Acid reflux, bowel problems	Weight gain or loss
Disruptive sleep, fears	Nightmares, obsessions
Sexual dysfunction	Avoid social gatherings
Anger outbursts	Compulsive behaviors
Bad, fitful dreams	

10. You may be greatly **tempted** to medicate, cover up, or escape from your pain through:

Alcohol/Pornography	Prescription drug misuse
Illegal drugs	Eating disorders
Adultery/Promiscuity	Avoiding home
Work-a-holism	Church-a-holism
Uncontrolled spending	Gambling
Too much or too little sleep	Isolation from others

The Apostle Paul reminds us that suffering, although painful, can serve a purpose. In Romans 5:3-5 he says,

"Not only so, but we also rejoice in our sufferings, because we know that suffering produces perseverance; perseverance, character; and character, hope. And hope does not disappoint us, because God has poured out his love into our hearts by the Holy Spirit, whom he has given us." We must understand that gaining strength of character and an abiding hope for the future comes at a cost."

Psalm 119:71 says learning God's ways through humility and discipline is profitable. It says,

"It was good for me to be afflicted so that I might learn your decrees."

Historian Roy Nichols concludes by stating:

"Pain is a great teacher, but most of us would rather learn some other way. We think that happiness comes from a perfect childhood and avoiding mistakes. We don't like that patched-up feeling that comes with each survival. We would like to be seamless, no patches, no scars. Cherish your hard-won depth and understanding. Some pain is required for the journey. The gifts you see are often disguised as problems. Patches bring strength, whether on our knees or in our hearts."

Small Group Discussion Chapter 9

1. What symptoms of the suffering family listed in this chapter have either you or someone you know personally experienced?

2. What are some additional symptoms not mentioned in this chapter that you believe indicate suffering, loss, hurt, and tension in a family?

3. What are some healthy and kind ways of interacting with and relating to marriages and families where suffering is present?

4. If possible, have each couple go off to be alone together to ask each other the following **Bridge Builder** question. Let your partner share while you listen attentively. When they are done, say to them the **Four Magic Words: "Please tell me more"**, and then listen lovingly again. Don't fix, don't correct, and don't disagree. Just listen attentively. Prize them. If time permits, summarize back to your partner what you believe you heard them say. In doing this, you demonstrate that you listened and that you value them. Then reverse roles and repeat the listening and sharing process.

Here is your seventh **Bridge Builder** question:

Please share your greatest need right now?

5. **(Note: Very important! Facilitator—be sure to take at least 10 minutes to break your group down into "couple to couple" groupings. Then ask them to share which Wave Makers and Wave Calmers from the "Growth Assignment" (page 142) they each circled and why. Take some time next week to continue if needed.)**

6. Please ask for prayer requests and then close in prayer.

Chapter 10

Oars and Life Jackets

When you get into a rowboat to go out onto a lake, you need two oars and some good life jackets. You are at the mercy of the elements without oars and in danger of drowning without life jackets. Yet, many marriages step down from the marriage altar having just exchanged vows and they launch out into their life together as if they had just gotten into rowboats without oars and life jackets. No wonder so many are lost in the storm.

When you get into the rowboat of marriage, after sitting down, the first thing you do is to firmly grab the left oar with your left hand. This left oar, we will call "hesed". This is a Hebrew word used about 250 times in the Old Testament.

The left oar is "Hesed"

In the Old Testament book of Hosea God commands a man by the same name to marry and thus love an unfaithful woman called Gomer. She even became a harlot after their marriage and Hosea has to buy her out of this sexual slavery. So much for her keeping her vows! The year was about 710 B.C. and God had called Hosea to be His prophet to the Northern Kingdom known as Israel.

Hosea 3:1-3 says, *"The LORD said to me, 'Go, show your love to your wife again, though she is loved by another and is an adulteress.* ***Love her as the LORD loves the Israelites, though they turn to other gods and love the sacred raisin cakes.'*** *So I bought her for fifteen shekels of silver and about a homer and a lethek of barley. Then I told her, 'You are to live with me many days; you must not be a prostitute or be intimate with any man, and I will live with you.'"* (Bold added)

Now in Hosea 2:19-20, God reveals to us the type of love He has for His children (Israel) and therefore the type of love Hosea is to demonstrate through obedience to God toward the unlovable, wretched Gomer. He was not asked to feel "in love" or to experience romantic warm fuzzies, but rather to show love.

Hosea 2:19-20 reads, *"I will betroth you to me forever; I will betroth you in righteousness and justice, in* **love** *and compassion. I will betroth you in faithfulness, and you will acknowledge the LORD."* (Bold added)

This love is "hesed". Charles Ryrie in the NIV Study Bible (p. 1203) writes, "It means loyal, steadfast, or faithful love and stresses the idea of a belonging together of those involved in the love relationship. Here it connotes God's faithful love for

His unfaithful people." You see, by Hosea choosing to obey God's command to unconditionally show mercy, kindness, and unwavering commitment to Gomer who did not deserve it, Israel would now have a "real life" model of God's unending, unmerited, unwavering love and mercy toward them.

Likewise, in Psalm 21:6,7, King David writes a powerful message to us: *"Surely you have granted him eternal blessings and made him glad with the joy of your presence. For the king trusts in the LORD; through the* ***unfailing love*** *of the Most High he will not be shaken."* (Bold added. This is the Hebrew word, "Hesed")

God's love will never fail you even when you fail Him. He will never leave or forsake you. Remember this. You are prone to failure. He is not. That is good news! You, oh Christian, are the glad recipient of God's everlasting, unconditional favor and uncondemnable kindness. His "hesed" for you is because of Him, not you. In His eyes, you, daughter or son of God, are innocent of all charges. You have been washed by the blood of the Lamb. You are holy and precious to Him. Amazing, isn't it? Treat your mate the way God treats you.

You are to demonstrate this same "hesed" love toward your mate. The world is watching. The world is searching for evidence that the God of the Bible is real and that His love for His children is unconditional and everlasting. When you honor God and love your mate as Hosea loved Gomer and as God loves His children, others will be drawn to the Lord Jesus Christ. Souls will be robbed from Hell, souls will be saved, and the numbers in Heaven will be increased. Now you know why Satan wants to isolate and destroy your marriage. People are looking at your marriage to see if Jesus and the Bible are real!

The Devil Plots To Destroy Your Marriage!

Imagine for a moment that you are sitting in your boat on the water at night. You are about 10 feet from shore. You are shining a big, bright, high intensity flashlight onto an object on the beach. The object is a big, filthy, scrappy porcupine. For illustration only, let us assume your mate is that porcupine. Even when the porcupine becomes unfriendly, or tries to seek the darkness, your high beam flashlight just follows it wherever it goes or whatever it does. The flashlight shines upon the object. This light is in no way dependent on anything the porcupine does or does not do. The porcupine cannot escape the light.

Your mate cannot escape your **love.** As God's son or daughter, you can never escape His love or His grasp. His "hesed" love for you goes wherever you go. His "hesed" love is unconditional. God's love for you is not dependent on your miserable ability to earn it or maintain it. You deserve Hell. God gives you Heaven. Your mate deserves Hell. You give him Heaven!

If you want to please God and bring honor to Him, "hesed" your mate. If you want the world to see the light and truth of Jesus, "hesed" your mate. If you want to bless your children, and smack the devil in the face, "hesed" your mate. Do you desire that the "Hope of The Ages" reaches out to the lost, the unloved, and the lonely? If so, "hesed" your mate. If you want everyone to know how God loves His children, "hesed" your mate. If Heaven is in your heart and blessing eternity your passion, then receive God's "hesed" and pass it on to your mate.

The Right Oar is "Agape"

After you have gotten a firm grasp on the left oar with your left hand, now grasp the right oar with your right hand. "Hesed" is Hebrew and Hebrew is the language used in the Old Testament. "Agape", on the other hand, is Greek and Greek is the main language of the New Testament. The right oar is "agape".

It was just before the Passover Feast and the evening meal was being served. The disciples were gathered around. Judas, the one who was to betray the Lord Jesus, had just taken a dipped piece of bread from Jesus (a symbolic act of beloved friendship). After Judas took the bread, he left quickly to betray Him.

We pick up with Jesus sharing with His intimate friends, His disciples, minus one, Judas. He says, in John 13: 34,35, *"A new command I give you: **Love** one another. As I have **loved** you, so you must **love** one another. By this all men will know that you are my disciples, if you **love** one another."* (Bold added)

The bold words in the Greek are all the same word: "Agape". This is not a reference to human love, sensual love, or brotherly love. This is the true love of God. Nothing manufactured by man comes close. It is God's way of treating His beloved children. "Agape" is heartfelt, demonstrated action that involves undeserved benevolence, tender loving kindness, and is always charitable even in the face of betrayal and rejection. "Agape" is both gracious and merciful when grace and mercy are the last things you would expect. The very nature of "Agape" is to issue forth boundless gushings of grace and mercy where scourging and judgment would normally be expected and deserved.

Applying this to marriage, if you want to obey God, then you must "agape" your mate as God continually "agapes" you. Any other choice is disobedience and sin. To get a richer view of this "agape", God's matchless supernatural love, let us look at Romans 5:8.

"But God demonstrates his own love for us in this: While we were still sinners, Christ died for us."

Do you see it mates? God does not just talk or write about true love, he demonstrates it with real sacrificial action. While your mate may deserve to be flogged, egged, or sentenced to cold leftovers, you demonstrate the very "agape" God demonstrates unto you. You may feel he deserves to be couched. You might feel like kicking him out of your bedroom, slamming your door for effect, and then inflicting guilt through pouting and silence. Instead, you choose to grace him and welcome him to the warmth and safety of your bedroom. You do not give him what he deserves. You give him God's love.

Don't take it the wrong way. If your mate is in sin bondage or is abusive or reckless, tough love and accountability are in order. But remember this. Aren't you glad God does not give you what you deserve or treat you in light of your inconsistent, less than desirable track record as a Christian?

If you are going to grab this right oar in your rowboat, do it decisively and irrevocably. Do it now by faith and action. Be men and women of grace and mercy. Like God, be gracious to your mate. Give him or her that which he or she can never earn. Like God, show mercy to your mate. Withhold from your mate that which he or she deserves. If he deserves flogging, demonstrate forgiveness. If she does not measure up, treat her as if she has more than surpassed your wildest expectations. You need to employ both the left and the right oars: "Hesed" and "Agape".

Since you naturally possess neither, humbly ask God to enable you to increase and abound in His love toward the rest of us who, like you, are stumbling and fumbling on the surface of this earth until we, the forgiven, finally reach the shores of Heaven. "Agape" says to your mate, "Honey, I love you just the way you are. You don't have to improve. You don't have to become a better Christian spouse. You have fully arrived in my heart. Even if you get worse, it is OK with me." 1 Thessalonians 3:12 reads, *"May the Lord make your love increase and overflow for each other and for everyone else, just as ours does for you."*

One Good Life Jacket

Let us imagine that you and your mate are vacationing in Paris, France and you are each having your own little picnic on opposite shores of the Seine River. You have your blanket spread out on the left river bank. You have found a nice shady spot under a big sycamore tree. You have your bucket of chicken, potato salad, chips, pickles, grapes, soda, and all the rest. Amazingly, your precious mate has a similar blanket with goodies spread out across the river on the right river bank.

Your tendency is to shout across the river, "Hey, come on over, eat and drink with me! Come, listen to me and see life from my side of the river. See life from my point of view for once!" This attitude is what destroys good marriages. It says, "You exist to hear me out, and meet my needs!" What is needed here is empathy. This is when you choose to act selflessly and your passion is to comfort, side with, and encourage the other person. **Empathy** is one good life jacket to have with you at all times! The heart of empathy is brokenness and humility, thinking of yourself less.

The Lord Jesus will prompt you to empathize with your mate. There you are sitting on your nice picnic blanket on your side of the river. Since it is "your side", you naturally think it is the best side. You think your way of looking at things and your view of the river is best. However, you choose to please the Lord by leaving the safe and proud comfort of your blanket and your side of the river. You choose to get up (even when you'd rather not), and walk over the little half moon bridge to the other side of the river.

You then shock your mate by asking permission to join her picnic experience. Your heart's desire is to quietly sit down on her blanket, eat her food with her, and listen to her side of the story. Your passion is not to be right or to win. Your passion is to care, to understand, and know a wee bit of what it is like to see and taste life from her perspective…from her side of the river.

When you minister empathy, Christ is in control. Your ears enlarge, your emotional drawbridge is lowered, and your mouth shrinks away. Of course, this repulses your flesh. That is OK. Die to your flesh. Let it go.

An empathetic dialogue might go something like this:

"You know honey, I have not been very attentive toward you lately with work and all. I guess I have wanted you to revolve around my world and my needs more than the reverse. I am truly sorry. Please forgive me. I want to now give you my undivided attention. I am all ears."

Here you may ask any of a number of meaningful questions that build and heal rather than tear down and destroy such as, *"Honey, what would you say your greatest need is right now?"* or *"When was the last time you really felt loved by me?"*

Then as she is sharing, you simply listen attentively, nodding your head, keeping tender eye contact. When she is done sharing, you share four magic words that most women from cradle to grave never hear, **"Please tell me more."** Now after she picks her jaw up from hitting the floor, you again listen so as to understand and experience her perspective.

Now men you will love this! After she has shared all she can, then you rephrase what she just shared with you in your own words because you want to understand her correctly. You start out with something like, *"Now Honey, I want to make sure I fully appreciate and understand what you are saying…that I get it right. So, is it true, that you feel your greatest need is to have regular times throughout the week where we share, listen to, debrief, and encourage one another so we can become closer as a couple?"*

Then, wife, you lovingly let him know how accurate his summary was and clarify anything he missed. You, husband, summarize again so as to get it right as close to 100% as you can. When this happens, your mate begins to experience being valued, listened to, and treasured. Oneness occurs. Christ shines through to the lost, the unloved, and the lonely.

Remember the key litmus paper test for empathy in your marriage is this:

If the Lord Jesus is first in your life, then your mate will experience being treasured and central in your heart. Your marriage will be a warm, kind, and inviting place to be.

A marriage without empathy becomes nothing more than a cold business arrangement between two people. Empathy says, "I will show you I care. You will experience attentive focus. You and your views will be respected, heard, and prized."

Another Good Life Jacket

Take a good look at your mate. Are you hoping he will improve? Are you working at trying to change or fix her? Or have you zeroed in on some faults, failures, weaknesses, or foibles about him that cause you to want to reject him? Let us go back to the Garden of Eden for a moment. God had made Adam and then caused Him to fall asleep. Then God took one of Adam's ribs from his side and fashioned his helpmate Eve.

Can you imagine the joyful expectancy God the Fashioner, God the Provider must have felt as He caringly found the right moment to present her as a gift to Adam? Now if you were God, how would you feel if when God presented Eve, Adam, while peering at her with a raised thumb, retorted back with, "She's not bad God, but do you have anything back in the stock room with longer legs, and oh yea, do you have any red heads?" Now ask yourself how Eve would feel. Read in the second chapter of Genesis what really happened.

"18The LORD God said, "It is not good for the man to be alone. I will make a helper suitable for him." 19Now the LORD God had formed out of the ground all the beasts of the field and all the birds of the air. He brought them to the man to see what he would name them; and whatever the man called each living creature, that was its name. 20So the man gave names to all the livestock, the birds of the air and all the beasts of the field.

But for Adam no suitable helper was found. 21So the LORD God caused the man to fall into a deep sleep; and while he was sleeping, he took one of the man's ribs and closed up the place with flesh. 22Then the LORD God made a woman from the rib he had taken out of the man, ***and he brought her to the man.*** (**Bold** added)

[23]The man said, "This is now bone of my bones and flesh of my flesh; she shall be called 'woman,' for she was taken out of man."

Adam's basic response was something like, "Holy Cow! Woooooooooo Mannnnnnnn! (That is where the word Wo-man = "woman" came from. Smile) Va Voo Pa! Where have you been all my life? You are exactly what I need!"

Why do you think Adam unconditionally received her as God's custom designed gift and helpmate? There can be only one reason. Adam trusted in his Provider, not the provision. So another good life jacket to have is: **Trust fully in God, your Provider, and don't question His provision.**

Now if a couple mutually understands they complete one another and they both possess a solid trust that God provides good gifts and never makes mistakes, they now have a good and God-pleasing reason to cut the apron strings and dependencies on parents and totally cling to one another. Genesis 2:24 states:

"For this reason a man will leave his father and mother and be united to his wife, and they will become one flesh."

Please listen carefully, if the devil can trick you into seeing your mate and union as a mistake, then he has won. If he hinders you from trusting God, the Provider, and thus prevents you from unconditionally receiving your mate as a wonderful gift from God, then the devil has established a beachhead or stronghold in your home. One of you will fail to leave your parents, and then the in-law wars will begin.

The one who has failed to leave parents and cleave to his or her mate will play a miserable tug of war trying to please everyone. This mate will end up displeasing and disobeying God, the Father, and marital discord and isolation will result.

Remember This Truth!

Men and women, once you are married, you are one flesh with your mate; God's chosen one for you. You are not one flesh with your parents. You are not one flesh with your children. You are not one flesh with brothers, sisters, or anyone else in the world. Therefore, let no one or nothing get in between you two who have become one. The devil and his legions will work relentlessly on sneaking a wedge in between the two of you. Your relationship with your mate is more important and must come before your relationship with parents, in-laws, children, church, friends, co-workers, or siblings.

Once again be reminded that I Peter 5:8,9 says:

"Be self-controlled and alert. Your enemy the devil prowls around like a roaring lion looking for someone to devour. Resist him, standing firm in the faith, because you know that your brothers throughout the world are undergoing the same kind of sufferings."

Be prepared for his subtle attacks. Be prepared for full frontal onslaughts. Stand firm, stay the course, cling to Christ, His Word, and to your mate at all cost!

Never Give Up!

Small Group Discussion — Chapter 10

1. Why do you think the devil is plotting to destroy your marriage? In what ways might you become a threat to advancing His agenda?

2. God commands us to love one another as He loves us. If this is true and we choose obedience, what will our mate experience if we choose to "hesed" and "agape" him or her?

3. How do you think God will respond when we obey His command to do this?

4. What would it look like if you showed empathy toward your mate and their struggles, foibles, problems, and shortcomings?

5. Share why the art of listening is more powerful than talking. Why do you think God gave you two ears and only one mouth?

6. Why do you think most husbands and wives have never heard the **Four Magic Words, "Please tell me more."**?

7. If attentive listening requires love, humility, and patience, what does self-focused talking require?

8. If possible, have each couple go off to be alone together to ask each other the following **Bridge Builder** question. Let your partner share while you listen attentively. When they are done, say to them the **Four Magic Words: "Please tell me more"**, and then listen lovingly again. Don't fix, don't correct, and don't disagree. Just listen attentively. Prize them. If time permits, summarize back to your partner what you believe you heard them say. In doing this, you demonstrate that you listened and that you value them. Then reverse roles and repeat the listening and sharing process.

Here is your eighth **Bridge Builder** question:

What could I do to be more considerate so that you would feel more love, valued, or listened to?

9. Please ask for prayer requests and then close in prayer.

Chapter 11

Plan Ahead!

Have you ever been caught out on a lake in a small boat when it starts to really rain?

We have wonderful friends who own a rustic two story home located down a romantic wooded hill right on Lake Winnipesaukee, New Hampshire.

There are no televisions. It has those wide boards for the wood floor and is stocked full of old books, cozy over stuffed chairs, puzzles, and board games. Built out over the water is a large screened porch with a long wooden table, Adirondack chairs, and even a bed for dozing. If you need to unwind, this is the place. It is a peaceful, relaxed get-a-way.

The last time we visited, they took us on a speed boat trip across the lake. We traveled more than five miles to reach our destination. After several relaxed hours of dining and milling around the shops, we headed home. As soon as we started back, we noticed that the sky behind us had quickly become dark purple. A large storm was approaching rapidly heading right for us. We had not planned on this!

The temperature dropped, the wind picked up, and raindrops began to fall. Steve, who is normally jovial, suddenly became serious. He said something like, "Hang on to your hats!" He pushed the throttle fully forward and headed toward home with great speed. We said more than a few prayers out loud! This dark and ferocious storm was gaining on us. The intense sheet of rain seemed just a few hundred yards behind us.

This crazy storm followed us all the way back home. As soon as we secured the boat and got inside, the heavy winds and rain engulfed us. It was so dark it seemed like night! We gave thanks to the Lord for sparing us from getting really drenched.

We should have checked the weather report. We should have been better prepared. Like preparing for approaching weather conditions, Barbara and I are convinced that married couples of all ages should be better prepared for managing their personal finances. This is called financial stewardship.

Since this is not a book primarily dealing with Christian financial management, we will only cover key elements.

Most of the couples that come in to see us for marital and family counseling are struggling with several problems. Practically speaking, about 90% of all couples that we see are also battling severely over personal finances, poor stewardship, lack of training, and self-discipline. They spend more than they make.

In the area of biblical stewardship, it is vital to understand that the 100% of the money and possessions you have or will receive are given to you by God. Therefore, have the responsibility to demonstrate godly, balanced stewardship in regard to all that God has entrusted to you. Many people think 90% of what they make and own is theirs and the rest is God's.

This is how the devil lies to us. Hear us clearly dear friends. You must refute this lie and choose to live your life in all areas including personal finances according to "that which is written in God's Holy Scriptures." The Christian marriage that is ruled by the Lord Jesus Christ will honor and obey His Holy Word, the Bible.

1. **All that you are and have is a gift from God.** He expects you to wisely manage all that has been entrusted to you. One hundred percent belongs to God. You will either be a wise or a poor steward of it. You will either flounder irresponsibly in the area of personal stewardship or you will seek wise counsel and manage what you have as a gift.

2. **It is wise to get help.** If you are struggling in this area and have more than $1,000 in credit card debt, we urge to get help from a financial counselor from church or the community. We endorse Crown Ministries and any books written by Larry Burkett. Also computer software such as Quicken or the Principal Plan can be of great help.

3. **First, you must learn to balance your checkbook each and every month.** Without this, you are floating aimlessly in the Bermuda Triangle! You also need to develop a plan that looks both to the short term (this month up to 12 months) and to the long term (to the end of your

retirement years). This is crucial since many of you will be living into your late 80's and even the 90's. Your **Personal Financial Plan** should have three sections:

- A Spending Plan
- A Giving Plan
- A Saving plan

4. **Test God? Yes, test God!** In the simplest of terms, a good target is to gratefully give back to God at least 10% of the 100% He entrusts to you so the work of the Lord can go forth. The key is this: God loves a marriage that gives cheerfully, sacrificially, abundantly, and secretly. When in doubt, give. When you are needy, give. When you get a short paycheck or get laid off, give. Learn to give by faith with a grateful heart. When the Holy Spirit nudges you, give. Give in and out of season. Do not wait to get out of debt, give to the work of the Lord now. Perhaps the only place in Scripture where God challenges you to test Him is in Malachi 3:7-12:

   "7 Ever since the time of your forefathers you have turned away from my decrees and have not kept them. Return to me, and I will return to you," says the LORD Almighty.

   "But you ask, 'How are we to return?'

   8 "Will a man rob God? Yet you rob me.

   "But you ask, 'How do we rob you?'

   "In tithes and offerings. 9 You are under a curse-the whole nation of you-because you are robbing me. 10 Bring the whole tithe into the storehouse, that there may be food

in my house. ***Test me in this," says the LORD Almighty,*** *"and see if I will not throw open the floodgates of heaven and pour out so much blessing that you will not have room enough for it. [11]I will prevent pests from devouring your crops, and the vines in your fields will not cast their fruit," says the LORD Almighty. [12]"Then all the nations will call you blessed, for yours will be a delightful land," says the LORD Almighty."* (Bold added for emphasis)

Luke 6:38 is a great promise from God to you:

"Give, and it will be given to you. A good measure, pressed down, shaken together and running over, will be poured into your lap. For with the measure you use, it will be measured to you."

Simply put, you cannot out give God.

We want to stress that giving out of guilt because you think God will love you more is a wrong motive and certainly not true. What pleases God is learning to give back to Him by faith and with a thankful heart for all He has done for you.

5. **Avoid debt.** Make it your immediate and long range goal and passion to get out of and avoid debt. We know this is difficult especially for students taking out loans. But with God's help and your patient self-discipline the above-mentioned goal will serve you well in the long run. If you are in debt and most of you are, make plans to get out of debt as early as possible. In some cases, a person will pay twice as much for a purchase as the original price because of interest paid over the long haul.

6. **Spend each week or month less than you earn.** Avoid buying things on time. If you need, say, a couch for your family room, do not buy it on time with interest. This is the worst thing you can do. Rather, save up a bit each month (keep a written log of this) and when you have enough saved, then **pay cash.** You may have to sit on the floor or on pillows for awhile. So what? When you have saved for and then have that couch, it will be paid for. That will feel really good! Stay away from impulse buying. This is where you go to the mall on a Saturday and you waltz around from store to store having a great time. If you are disciplined in spending, this is usually not a problem. Most people are not, however. Many people see something they like and what do they do? You know what they do! **They pull out the plastic!** The average family's unpaid ongoing credit card debt is somewhere around $8,000! We know of some missionaries with credit card debt (abuse) of between $25,000 and $28,000!

7. **Pay off your credit card(s) each month in full.** This is our strong pleading: Get a handle on your credit cards today. If you must have one, it should be used rarely for things like emergencies. One of our daughters and her husband decided to be prudent. They obtained just one credit card with a limit of $1000.00 for emergencies. They say it helps them not to over spend. They have learned it is better to not have such a looming, ever present temptation nesting in their wallet or purse.

   I only use one for emergencies, gasoline, and paying for air travel. Barbara carries a few more like a J.C. Penny's card and a GAP card. Here is where self-discipline is essential. **We made a commitment long ago to pay off all credit card bills in full each month.** We have seen one couple with 12 cards all charged to their highest limits! They ended up divorced and bankrupt. If you cannot do this, get a scissors and cut them all up. You will be glad you did.

8. **Divide each paycheck compartmentally.** A great idea is to get help from a relative or close friend or as we have encouraged, someone from Crown Ministries. They will help you develop a plan. Barbara and I set aside, say $10 a month, $25 a month, or $50 a month for various needs that will come up down the road. For instance, we save $50 a month for our annual vacation. When the vacation time comes, the money is there. We do the same for Christmas gifts, car repairs and registration, house maintenance, property tax, income tax preparation, etc.

   Since I have to pay $100 a year in December in order to renew my Ordination certificate, we save $10 each month in our bank's savings account. Then in December, I have the $100 that has been building up all year plus I have an extra $20 for next year.

   We have 5 daughters. We promised each of them that we would contribute $1,500 toward their wedding. Now that is not much when you think of wedding costs these days, but with five daughters that is all we could do. We have been saving $25 a month for many months now. Three daughters are married. If and when a fourth gets married, we will be ready. As of today, we have $1,225 saved thus far. This plan really works!

   You should also get professional advice from a Certified Financial Advisor about setting money aside each pay check for your children's college / technical school costs and for retirement.

9. **Consider buying used cars.** There are arguments for both buying new and used cars. At this stage in our life, we will never buy a new car again! Once you drive it off the lot, it depreciates thousands of dollars in value. We buy only used cars. We save $25 here and $50 there. We recently paid cash for a used, four year old Buick with 53,000 miles on it. We paid one third the original sticker price. Our other vehicle is an 11 year old GMC 8 passenger van with over 210,000 miles on it. With 7 kids and college, this cargo transporter has been useful. It is also paid for. We have full insurance on the Buick and only liability insurance on the van. They do need regular repairs, tires, oil changes, new brakes, etc, but the good news is they are PAID FOR!

10. **Avoid loaning money to loved ones.** Our experience as biblical counselors is that it strains relationships in an unhealthy manner. If you want to give them money, great! But give without conditions. Give with absolutely no strings attached. Don't even keep a record of how much you give a loved one. We helped each of our children with some of their college expenses. However, we told them they would have to pay for the rest of their education. We know not all parents will be able to do this and that is understandable.

11. **Never take a second mortgage out on your house!** No matter what the need, refuse to do this! You are putting yourself in financial bondage in your later years. If you want to go on that big vacation, painstakingly save for it each and every month. Without self-discipline, poverty, debt, and strained relationships occur.

1. Discuss this: Stewardship is not a matter of the wallet. It is a matter of the heart.

2. Discuss what has happened to couples the small group knows (no names please) who have or who had no financial plan or little discipline in how to spend and manage their money.

3. Test God? Yes, test God! Have someone read Malachi 3:7-12 out loud while the rest of the small group members read silently and listen. Ask the group how many are willing to test God in this?

4. If faith is defined as, **"Choosing to live as though the Bible is true, regardless of circumstances, emotions, or cultural trends"** how will your view toward money and giving, change? What does it mean to give to God by faith with a grateful and trusting heart? Should you give sacrificially, hilariously, and abundantly only when you think you have enough money? Why or why not?

5. Since the average credit card debt for a typical American couple is around $8,000, how might this burden affect the stress level in a marriage? Will this heavy pressure tend to cause two marital rowboats to drift apart or draw close together? Why? What about you?

6. What does it look like to do everything in your power to get out and stay out of debt? Is it worth it? What are the consequences of getting into deeper debt?

7. If possible, have each couple go off to be alone together to ask each other the following **Bridge Builder** question. Let your partner share while you listen attentively. When they are done, say to them the **Four Magic Words: "Please tell me more"**, and then listen lovingly again. Don't fix, don't correct, and don't disagree. Just listen attentively. Prize them. If time permits, summarize back to your partner what you believe you heard them say. In doing this, you demonstrate that you listened and that you value them. Then reverse roles and repeat the listening and sharing process.

Here is your ninth **Bridge Builder** question:

What area of my life do you see as needing work or attention?

8. Please ask for prayer requests and then close in prayer.

Chapter 12

Let Your Lighthouse Shine

A few years ago, Barbara and I were invited to speak at a week long Tadmor Christian Family Camp in the Cascade Mountains in Oregon. They were very gracious and enabled us to fly our family out there as well.

We were up in the forested mountain region, with pristine lakes, and natural beauty all around us.

In the middle of the week, one of the kind ladies from the camp leadership team drove our family west to Newport, Oregon on the coast of the Pacific. We were astounded. Just two hours before, we were up in the mountains and now we were at sea level digging our toes into the sand and feeling the refreshing water swirl around our feet. While eating oysters in a rustic eatery built out over the water on stilts, we watched the sea lions play in the water by the rocks.

After lunch, she drove us to a famous lighthouse on a cliff overlooking the ocean. Words cannot describe the majestic beauty. God is an amazing Creator! It was windy and the sea gulls looked like they were flying stationary in one place. No doubt at night the bright beam of the light could be seen for many miles by those out at sea.

This lighthouse, along with others like it around the world, and the people who staff them, have been in rescues involving great heroism. One such true story is that of **The Grace Darling Rescue:**

> On September 7th, 1838, near the Farne Islands off the North Norththumberland Coast *{of Britain}*,... the 400 ton paddle steamship "Forfarshire" was on passage from Hull to Dundee when it struck rocks near to the Longstone Lighthouse, in a northern gale. The vessel broke in two almost immediately, and many passengers were drowned as the aft section quickly sank…Thirteen people…were able to scramble onto the Harcar Rock. About half a mile away, on the Longstone Lighthouse, were William Darling, his wife Thomasin and their youngest daughter Grace….At first light on the 8th, Grace spotted the wreck of the "Forfarshire" from her bedroom window, and alerted her family.
>
> As the light grew stronger, they could just make out the survivors huddled on the rocks. Grace and her father decided at once to attempt a rescue, and put out their 21-foot coble, rowing it through heavy seas towards the casualties. They could not take a direct route, having to avoid other rocks, and with tremendous skill and courage, managed to reach the rocks and rescue some of the survivors, who in turn helped row the coble back to

the lighthouse. Grace and her father decided to make a return trip to rescue those remaining, where they were also successfully saved and taken back to the lighthouse. Here they remained for 2 days due to the storms, being cared for by the Darling family.[2]

Their heroism and gallantry did not go unnoticed. Grace and her father both were awarded silver gallantry medals. Grace received additional gold medallions for her courage and bravery against difficult and overwhelming odds.

Your Family
God's Lighthouse To The World

Barbara and I want you to begin to see your marriage and family as His uniquely designed lighthouse of love, kindness, mercy, truth, and hospitality. As biblical counselors, we meet with hundreds of individuals, marriages and families that are so desperate for hope, for someone who cares. They will do almost anything to get help. We know God has called us to serve, comfort, and rescue them from the dark and stormy seas they have fallen into. If you look at the sea as a place where sin, pain, sorrow, and despair engulf lost and hurting souls, you will see that you too are called by God to shine His Light to reach out to them and bring them into safe harbors.

Jesus says to you this day…

"You are the light of the world. A city on a hill cannot be hidden. Neither do people light a lamp and put it under a bowl. Instead they put it on its stand, and it gives light to everyone in the house. In the same way, let your light shine before men, that they may see your good deeds and praise your Father in heaven." (Matthew 5:14-16)

I took some time and pondered that big lighthouse high up on that Oregon coastline. I noticed that the bright light shines outward, searching, offering hope to those doomed and struggling. It reaches out to those who have lost their bearings. Another interesting way of looking at that light is that it also draws in those ships like a homing beacon.

Not only are you commissioned to go out of your home to search out and reach those in need of compassion and truth, but you are also called to open your home and gladly welcome people in. This is called hospitality, the lost art in our dying post-modern culture.

God never intended that our being saved from sin, death, and hell would benefit only us.

Jesus has redeemed us so He can redeem others through us.

Of what value is a lighthouse that shines no light?

What about you? What about your marriage? What about your home? Is it a lighthouse shining compassion, and hospitality? Is it designed for self-focus and pleasure or is it ready at God's beckoning to leave the safety of your walls and go out and rescue those drowning in the sea muck of life? Consider God's desire for you in Exodus 9:16 which states:

"But I have raised you up for this very purpose, that I might show you my power and that my name might be proclaimed in all the earth."

Because you are God's marriage, we want to challenge you to start letting your Lighthouse light shine in three specific ways.

Let your servant light shine.

Jesus again is saying to you today…

"Not so with you. Instead, whoever wants to become great among you must be your servant, and whoever wants to be first must be your slave—just as the Son of Man did not come to be served, but to serve, and to give his life as a ransom for many." (Matthew 20:26-28)

The painful part about being a servant is that it requires humility. We don't like humility because it tends to be humiliating! You will know you are a servant when people start treating you like one. Not too many of us want that! How about you?

Note that a servant is:

- Vulnerable
- Surrendered
- Hospitable

The Apostle Paul, in his profound letter to the Roman Christians told them to:

"Share with God's people who are in need. Practice hospitality. Bless those who persecute you; bless and do not curse". (Romans 12:13,14)

We are asking you to join us in obeying God's Word and opening up your home for Bible Studies, neighborhood cookouts, and prayer gatherings. Consider temporarily housing missionaries who are visiting on furlough.

Do you desire to serve at your church or be served? Is it your tendency to complain about your church or show compassion and support to imperfect people there? Are you inclined to cutting and running when relationships become difficult? Remember this. You will never take on the yoke of servanthood and hospitality until you decide to get off your pity pot and ask God to give you a heart of gratitude. Only grateful hearts are hospitable hearts. Only grateful hearts facilitate healing.

Let your purity light shine.

The enemy of purity is happiness. This does not quite sound right so let us explain. Barbara and I counseled a nice middle-aged woman who was born in South East Asia. She came to us because although married, she was having an affair with another man where she worked. She was deeply sincere in her struggle.

We compassionately shared God's Word with her. She looked at us with tears forming and said, "But I juss wan be hoppy!" Because her goal is happiness, to our best knowledge she is still committing adultery. A. W. Tozer said, "It is better to die holy than to live happy."

The following scriptures apply:

"Flee the evil desires of youth, and pursue righteousness, faith, love and peace, along with those who call on the Lord out of a pure heart." (II Timothy 2:22)

"He who loves a pure heart and whose speech is gracious will have the king for his friend." (Proverbs 22:11)

"But among you there must not be even a hint of sexual immorality, or of any kind of impurity, or of greed, because these are improper for God's holy people." (Ephesians 5:3)

"How can a young man keep his way pure? By living according to your word. I seek you with all my heart; do not let me stray from your commands. I have hidden your word in my heart that I might not sin against you." (Psalm 119:9-11)

"Blessed are the pure in heart, for they will see God." (Matthew 5:8)

Let your mercy light shine.

If you recall, we defined "grace" as giving someone that which they do not deserve. "Mercy" is withholding that which someone does deserve. As a couple, be known for being merciful. Mercy is for those who are destitute. Do you have a growing love for the lost, the wretched, and those who deserve punishment? If not, ask God to help you. Show mercy to others.

Ponder the following Scriptures:

"While they were stoning him, Stephen prayed, 'Lord Jesus, receive my spirit.' Then he fell on his knees and cried out, 'Lord, do not hold this sin against them.' When he had said this, he fell asleep." (Acts 7:59,60)

"Mercy, peace and love be yours in abundance. Be merciful to those who doubt; snatch others from the fire and save them; to others show mercy, mixed with fear—hating even the clothing stained by corrupted flesh.". (Jude 1:2, 22,23)

"Be merciful, just as your Father is merciful." (Luke 6:36)

The final truth we want to share with you is very simple. In a Lighthouse marriage, we ask husbands and wives to make it your undying passion to follow the Lord Jesus and allow His amazing love to pour out on your mate that He has chosen for you from before the foundation of the world. In order to let your mercy light shine, you must help to relieve the suffering of others no matter who they are, where they come from, or what they have done. You must relieve the suffering even of those who have hurt you.

Husbands, lift up your wives!

Men, we charge you with the blessed mission of continually **lifting up** your wives. We are not talking about physically lifting them up, but rather spiritually and emotionally.

The Amplified Version of the Bible in Ephesians 5:25, 28, and 29 reads,

"Husbands, love your wives, as Christ loved the church and gave Himself up for her, For no man ever hated his own flesh, but nourishes and carefully protects and cherishes it, as Christ does the church."

Men, this is not an option or a suggestion. It is an order, a command from your God and he will hold you accountable to it. He will encourage you, inspect you, and help you obey it.

Wives, build up your husbands!

Now ladies, we charge you with the blessed mission of continually **building up** your husbands.

The Amplified Version of the Bible in Ephesians 5:33 reads:

"...and let the wife see that she respects and reverences her

husband- that she notices him,...honors him,...and admires him exceedingly."

Again, ladies, this is not based on whether or not you feel they deserve this. They don't. Apart from Christ, like you, they deserve Hell. But since Jesus gave you Heaven, you give your men Heaven. Focus on where they are even partially winning, not on where they are falling short. When you feel like batting them down, stop and choose to **build them up.**

Remember, women, submission is not being a slave or doormat. When Jesus chose to submit to His Heavenly Father in the Garden of Gethsemane, God's plan of redemption went forward. To submit is to voluntarily come under the authority of your husband in order to revere God. Being pleased and honored, God will give you a testimony to your family and to the world that Jesus is both alive and your wonderful Lord and Savior.

Biblical submission is reverently and respectfully looking out for your husband's best interests. You would never obey your husband if he asks you to do anything that would dishonor God or isolate you or others from godly fellowship. Thus, he is in contempt of God's court if he tries to demand that you stay home from church.

You do not lie for him to cover for any sin on his part such as drunkenness. You let him fall flat on his face and hit rock bottom. Submission also implies, ladies, that if your husband threatens or beats you, you quickly and forthrightly call 911 and throw him in jail for a while. Submission means you will desire God's holy best for him. He may not like your tough love, but God will. The Lord will honor you. When given the opportunity to talk bad about your husband, instead talk good about him.

Together, affirm your children!

You are commissioned by God to love, coach, nurture, and train your children in light of their God-fashioned bent. You are to train them through modeling and discipline to trust, love, and obey the Lord Jesus Christ.

You know that children are a gift from the Lord. They are precious and at times fragile. Other times they seem quite resilient. When they go out your door, perhaps onto a school bus, or eventually to service or college, you know the world will try to squeeze them into its mold. The world will use shame, performance, ridicule, bullies, back stabbers, gossip, sin bondage, ill-chosen friends, peer pressure, ungodly web sites, and the media to attempt to demoralize, defeat, and put down your kids.

If you are a mom or a dad, be firm, but fair and gracious. Since your kids receive an average of 17 negative put down "feel bad about yourself" messages a day, try to counteract this by making your home a safe haven. Ensure that a gracious, lighthearted, and affirming spirit is present. You have to have a few rules and you need to stick to them. We are strong believers in respect for authority. Kids need to learn to submit to authority that God has placed over them. Do not compromise on this. Be consistent and unified with your mate. Being inconsistent with your children will cause them to feel unloved and detached.

You need to know where they are, whom they are with, and what they are doing. When young, read to them and then read some more to them. Play with them, Wrestle with them. Get goofy with them. Pray with them at bed times. When they hit the teen years, some of them will test you for sure. You do not have to be their friend. You have to be their parent. If you can find a way, bless them with an affirming word. Believe in them.

Listen to them. Try not to over react in anger. It is tempting at times! Tell them that although trust is always earned and can be lost, your love for them is never earned. Your love is always unconditional.

Blending our family has been extremely difficult. Don't let anyone tell you it is easy. Barbara and I adopted two principles that helped to pull us through.

1. As mentioned earlier, what is best for our marriage will be best for the family and everyone else. We refused to allow our kids, in-laws, or anyone else to divide or isolate Barbara and me. We would not allow anyone to push our two rowboats away from each other.

2. We insisted that each family member treat each other with:

    - Respect
    - Honesty &
    - Kindness

    With nine people in our family we made many mistakes and failed at times by violating these principles. Can you imagine nine sinners in one home? However, we chose to stick to these principles, asked others for forgiveness frequently, and worked diligently at reconciliation.

Remember This Definition of Family Love

"**Forsaking** all resentment and past failure, **pursue** each family member with acceptance, encouragement, kindness, compassion, and forgiveness. Leave all results up to God."

Both words in "**bold**" are action verbs. They refer to continuous action that requires both sacrifice and a gut choice of the will that overrules emotions, feelings, and past hurts. This is the way Jesus loved us on His Cross. What would this world be like if He, instead, kept reminding us of how we have wronged Him? He commands us to keep no record of wrongs, (1 Corinthians 13:5), forgive others readily, and choose to love them regardless of their response or ability to earn such love. Family love never reminds others of their failures. But be wise! Do not let others take advantage of you or mistreat you. Be sure to set boundaries where necessary.

A lonely lantern carried on a moonless night deep in the woods will neither shine nor offer light to others unless fully lit. Likewise, a marriage and family who daily does not **forsake resentment** and **pursue with forgiveness** will remain dark, offering no hope or comfort to anyone.

A tender, closing thought…

One sunny late afternoon, Barbara and I were asked to meet secretly with a lady. She asked us to meet her way up high at the edge of this bluff where there was a clearing amidst the giant pine trees. There were some cut stumps of pine trees that we could sit on and from our secluded outlook, we could see for 50 miles as the sun slowly sank in the western sky. We were up quite high and it seemed that the Lord Himself was there with us. This dear lady who was very affluent confided in us that her husband was a C.I.A operative and had gotten too close to the drug lords. He was crossing over to a life of crime and was divorcing her. How's that for a quiet, secluded, moment in the woods?

We comforted and listened to her as she sobbed. We were with her for over an hour. It was just the three of us. Quietly and wonderfully, the presence, the assurance, and the peace of God overwhelmed us. We just sat there quietly with this hurting lady and God took over. We all knew He was with us and that there was nothing to worry about. This was a Divine Appointment.

Get quiet with Jesus. Seek Him and He will be found by you. He will help you and He will strengthen and equip your marriage. Be of good courage! He will reveal His mission for you.

[2]Royal National Lifeboat Institution. "The Grace Darling Rescue." *Seahouses Lifeboats Online*, 2005. <http://www.seahouseslifeboat.org.uk/gd.html>.

Small Group Discussion Chapter 12

1. Since there is no marriage (a man and a woman) in Heaven, and certainly none in Hell, why do you think God ordained marriage between one man and one woman here on earth? Why not just live together and have children without God's plan and blessing? Discuss this in light of our Lord's passion for lost, hurting and undiscipled souls still on earth. What is the mission for God's marriages here on earth?

2. Discuss what it means to **let your lighthouse shine**.

3. In light of the above question, which of the following discussed in this chapter spoke to you the most? Why?

   - Let your servant light shine
   - Let your purity light shine
   - Let your mercy light shine

4. Husbands please give one example how you will lift up your wives this week. Likewise, wives please give one example how you will build up your husbands.

5. Discuss ways in which you affirm your children. What works? (Note: Some couples may not have children and some may not be able to have them. Please be sensitive.)

6. Discuss the definition of **Family Love. "Forsaking all resentment and past failure, pursue each family member with acceptance, encouragement, kindness, compassion, and forgiveness. Leave all results up to God."**

7. If possible, have each couple go off to be alone together to ask each other the following **Bridge Builder** question. Let your partner share while you listen attentively. When they are done, say to them the **Four Magic Words: "Please tell me more"**, and then listen lovingly again. Don't fix, don't correct, and don't disagree. Just listen attentively. Prize them. If time permits, summarize back to your partner what you believe you heard them say. In doing this, you demonstrate that you listened and that you value them. Then reverse roles and repeat the listening and sharing process.

Here is your tenth **Bridge Builder** question:

If there was one prayer request that God would most certainly grant about our relationship, what would it be?

8. Finally discuss what you gained from completing **The Freedom Exercise** (page 133).

9. Please ask for prayer requests and then close in prayer.

Freedom Exercise

"I will walk about in freedom,
for I have sought out your precepts."

Psalm 119:45

Your Great Commandment / Great Commission focused marriage is being plotted against as you read this. The devil specializes in enslavement. He loves to isolate! He's got you in his sights. He wants you and your mate to experience real bondage, shame, and defeat. He is out to destroy you and your home. We are not going to let that happen!

Have each couple go to a different part of your home (if possible) and work together through "**The Three Steps to Freedom**".

Step #1

Release Your Guilt.

"Devil" means slanderer. Satan is the Accuser of the Brethren. He wants you feeling guilty and condemned all of the time! Satanic guilt starts a **Death Cycle**:

1. You sin, mess up, or just blow it.

2. You condemn yourself. Satan and his demons cheer you on.

3. You then despair and beat yourself up without mercy.

4. You flee, hide, or just give up. Your smile covers your despair. You isolate yourself from your mate only to set yourself up to sin or fail again.

5. This vicious cycle starts all over again.

Now when you are truly guilty of sin, the Holy Spirit within you allows you to feel and experience His conviction in order to motivate you to **repent** of your sin (agree with God, turn away from your sin, and fully surrender to His Lordship again). There will be no sweetness in your marriage until you do.

It is conviction from a loving God. He has your **best** in mind when He employs it.

God's conviction is like a **Life Preserver**:

1. God's conviction is **RESCUING**.
2. God's conviction is **RESTORING**.
3. God's conviction is **HEALING**.

GOD'S CONVICTION: THE WONDERFUL LIFE PRESERVER

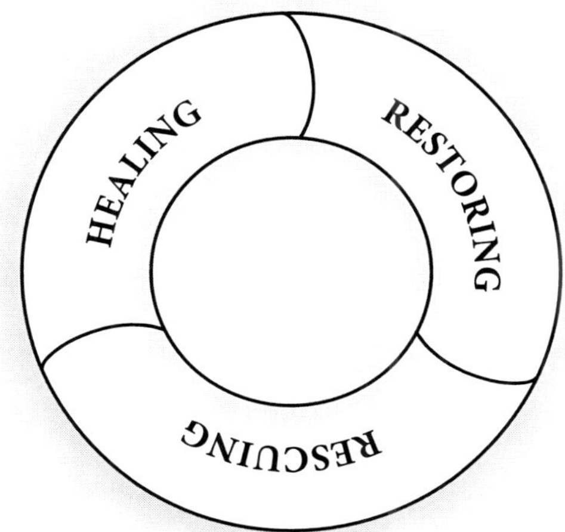

As a child of God, **picture yourself drowning** in a sea of sin, despair, self-examination, or disbelief. Jesus is not on some condemning tower looming over you, looking down at you with piercing, shaming, and condemning eyes. Jesus came to save the world, not condemn it.

Instead, I see Jesus in a **sturdy rescue ship**. He not only throws you His Life Preserver (Conviction), but He, Himself, jumps in after you. Because you know His motive is to save and to care deeply, you will quickly want to receive His help. You are helpless without it. He lifts you up and out. Together read Psalm 40:1-3:

> [1]*I waited patiently for the LORD; he turned to me and heard my cry.*
>
> [2]*He lifted me out of the slimy pit, out of the mud and mire; he set my feet on a rock and gave me a firm place to stand.*

[3]He put a new song in my mouth, a hymn of praise to our God. Many will see and fear and put their trust in the LORD.

He takes you to the warmth and safety of His **ship of restored fellowship** and He puts dry clothes on you, feeds you, and smiles upon you!

This is a picture of a **Life Cycle:**

1. You sin, mess up, or blow it.
2. You experience God's healing conviction. (John 16:8)
3. Jesus is jumping in to rescue and restore you. (Forgiveness & Fellowship)
4. Not wanting to choke in the drowning sea any longer that you have to, you quickly cry out to Jesus for help and forgiveness.
5. Instead of hiding, you receive His loving, affirming embrace and you then want to remain safe in His care. Fellowship restored; isolation destroyed.

Any remaining guilt you feel apart from the Holy Spirit's conviction is destructive, hurtful, and **enslaving!** It is not from God.

Take turns with your partner reading out loud the following verses:

☐ *Then I acknowledged my sin to you and did not cover up my iniquity. I said, "I will confess my transgressions to the LORD"—and you forgave the guilt of my sin.*
(Psalm 32:5)

☐ *You are my hiding place; you will protect me from trouble and surround me with songs of deliverance.* (Psalm 32:7)

☐ *Therefore, there is now no condemnation for those who are in Christ Jesus,* (Romans 8:1)

☐ *If we confess our sins, he is faithful and just and will forgive us our sins and purify us from all unrighteousness.* (1 John 1:9)

Individually "√" the "☐" of the verse that frees your heart up the most. Then, together, discuss why you checked your verse.

If you have any unconfessed sin, please privately confess it to the Lord right now.

Step #2

Release Your Burdens.

Do you insist on carrying your own burdens? The Lord did not design you to carry burdens for too long.

It is also true that Henry Ford did not design the automobile to fly.

Cast all your anxiety on him because he cares for you. (1 Peter 5:7)

The American Heritage Dictionary defines "cast" as:

1. To throw or fling.
2. To turn or direct.
3. To deposit.
4. To release.

Your Heavenly Father reserves the right to carry your burdens. Sometimes He does this through other people. If you have burdens and troubles that are causing you anxiety, please cast them to your Father right now…… He is waiting.

Step #3

Release Others From Your Judgments.

If you are holding grudges, stewing, fretting, or harboring resentment and bitterness toward someone dead or alive, you are in sin, and therefore are in bondage.

If you remain offended by someone's action or attitude toward you, then your heart is filled with **judgment**. God wants to fill it with **mercy**.

Take turns reading the following verses out loud with your partner:

> *Be merciful, just as your Father is merciful. Do not judge, and you will not be judged. Do not condemn, and you will not be condemned. Forgive, and you will be forgiven.* (Luke 6:36-37)

> *For the LORD is our judge, the LORD is our lawgiver, the LORD is our king; it is he who will save us.* (Isaiah 33:22)

> *Be kind and compassionate to one another, forgiving each other, just as in Christ God forgave you.* (Ephesians 4:32)

When you forgive someone, they don't have to ask to be forgiven or even apologize.

You are to **release** them from your requirement that they should somehow suffer or pay for the injustice and wounds they caused. You are to agree to **endure** the injustice, unfairness, and wrongful suffering that they have caused.

Jesus, on the cross, agreed to endure the sin and injustice you inflicted on Him. So you must do likewise to others who have hurt you if you are to call yourself Christian. Let them **go free**. You must release them from your judgment if you say you love God.

Is there someone – a parent, relative, mate, ex-mate, brother, sister, friend, son, daughter, a boss, your pastor, your church, or yourself—that you need to release from your judgment?

If so, please release them now.

Your humble prayer might start like…

Heavenly Father,

I release __________________________ from my judgment.

I forgive them fully. I can do this because You forgave me and You are able to work in their lives much better than I am. Thanks for freeing me from this bondage.

Thanks for forgiving me for holding on to this as long as I have. I love you!

In Jesus' name,

____________________ ____________________

(date) *(signature)*

Please use this prayer format to forgive each person or organization specifically one at a time.

Wave Makers and Wave Calmers

Wave Makers are carnal, destructive roles that people either assume or adopt in their marriage and family relationships. They are dysfunctional, sinful, and oppose the purposes of God. The devil encourages them.

If Wave Makers are not dealt with, they will rapidly push your two marriage rowboats far apart. Isolation, discouragement, deception, and destruction will inevitably result.

Wave Calmers are roles pleasing to God. They honor God and His Word. Mates that adopt these are wise, godly, and Spirit-led. They will help fulfill the purposes of God.

Your inclination might be to assign some Wave Makers to your mate. This would be to Satan's delight.

Please do not do that.

Growth Assignment:

As you read the **Wave Makers** and the **Wave Calmers**, choose one from each category **(circle them)** that speaks to your heart the most. Be prepared to tell why if you are meeting in a small group or class setting.

Wave Makers: I circled number _______

Wave Calmers: I circled number _______

Ask only that the Lord examine your heart. Ask Him to use this information in your life in order to serve and love your mate in a more balanced, healthy, and godly manner. (This material is adopted from **Home To Home: Passing On Five Cornerstones of Christian Marriage** by Jim and Barbara Grunseth, published by Campus Crusade for Christ, New Life Resources, Peachtree City, GA)

Wave Makers

1. Too Nice Mate
2. Overprotective, Oversacrificial Mate
3. Nonprotective Mate
4. Present, but Absent Mate
5. Subtle Cyanide Mouth
6. Insult for Insult Mates
7. Emotional Hook Mate
8. Codependent Mate
9. Controlling Mate
10. Two-Faced Mate
11. Shaming Mate
12. Christian Mate Controlled by the Flesh

Wave Calmers

1. Christian Mate Controlled by the Spirit
2. Suffering Mate
3. Parent-Honoring Mates
4. Submission
5. Tough Love
6. Gracing Mate

Wave Makers

1. TOO NICE MATE

This is an overly passive "milk toast" mate who demonstrates a low self-worth by almost always giving in to the whims, desires, and ideas of the other mate.

Example: "John, where would you like to take me out for dinner tonight?" "Well, Gee, Mary, I'll go wherever you want to go." "John, I'd rather have you (lead once) choose." "Oh Mary, let's go wherever you would be the happiest!" Mary, half out of her mind by now, "I think I'm sick to my stomach, John! Let's not go out at all!"

Avoid being a "Too Nice Mate." Demonstrate some backbone once in a while, John. Take the lead a little. Add some mystique and let her know that you are taking her out.

2. OVERPROTECTIVE, OVERSACRIFICIAL MATE

This mate is imbalanced in sacrificing all of his or her needs and desires. This mate is one who goes overboard on protecting his or her mate.

Example: "Tom, let's face it. You don't like to visit my parents. You also don't like me going out for lunch with Karen, my best friend. So I'll tell my parents that we just won't be coming over... hardly ever. And I'll also stop seeing Karen."

"Sandy! You'd love me that much?" "Yes, Tom. Jesus died for me so I'll die socially and emotionally for you..." In the meantime, Tom's selfish irresponsibility is enlarged and several important needs of Sandy's will now go unmet. This will lead to an ingrown, tense-filled relationship that will lead to certain troubles, burnout, and resentment.

3. NONPROTECTIVE MATE

This mate is imbalanced and lacks the proper self-control to properly protect.

Example: "Ramón, I just can't take it any longer! Every time we go to your parents' home, your mother belittles and embarrasses me right in front of our kids and you! I feel so vulnerable, unprotected, and defenseless. Ramón, you just seem to sit there and let them get away with it. Where is your allegiance to me?"

"Well, Maria, I just don't know what to do. I don't want you feeling threatened and I sure wouldn't want to hurt or offend my parents. They've been so good to us."

Note: If Ramón does not choose to take command and confront his parents in love, his parents will continue to show disrespect toward Maria. Their marriage will be in deep trouble. Ramón is a fence sitter. He needs to be decisive. With little explanation, he needs to respectfully tell his parents that if such behaviors continue, consequences will follow. If he gets trapped into always having to explain his decisions, his parents will be able to control him from a distance. Ramón does not need to give explanations. He simply needs to lead and protect his lady, his wife.

4. PRESENT, BUT ABSENT MATE

This mate may be home near the family but is certainly not "with" the family. His mind is constantly on work, office drama, his own sagging self-image, church responsibilities, phone calls to return, or the meeting tomorrow.

Perhaps he has become "one" with the personal computer, video games, or the couch as in COUCH POTATO, with attention to the "one-eyed Trojan Horse," THE TV. This mate may feel that he deserves all these breaks today while, in reality, he is carrying on an affair with the above mentioned activities. The one married to such a selfish person goes bananas after awhile!

He actually says, "Ah...see, Martha! I didn't bring any work home tonight from the office!" The problem is that he brought home his "mental" briefcase.

5. SUBTLE CYANIDE MOUTH

This mate's words produce discouragement, despair, and blame. Her words cut instead of heal. She uses words that bring down instead of lift up. She exercises her mouth to try to catch others doing something wrong instead of catching them doing something right, even partially right.

She nags and loves to use "always" and "never." "YOU ALWAYS...!" or "YOU NEVER...!" She thinks she is good at telling someone the truth. Often, though, she is giving "piercing, truthful" feedback without love. She thinks she is right because she is telling a truth the person deserves or needs to hear.

If you have to correct, reprove, or rebuke someone, be sure to give your message enveloped in loving kindness. Timing, respect, and understanding are everything. Ask yourself if your goal is to "put down" or "build up." Then share, with the Lord directing you.

6. INSULT FOR INSULT MATES

These mates were probably raised in homes where family members subconsciously returned disrespect and insults to each other as a habitual way of life.

When one mate (the sending mate) insults, belittles, or degrades, it becomes a natural, carnal reflex for the receiving mate to send back a similar insult, usually one that will inflict the most pain and damage. This destructive cycle can continue on for years and can be passed on through future generations. We see this on TV shows and in world news every day: Someone treads on your turf so you tread on theirs! After all, they deserve it. Right? Revenge has become the international past time. Just take a look at what is going on in the Middle East?

Example: Joe says to Jane, "Thanks a lot! You're never interested in the pressures I'm facing at work! All you want me around for is to get a bunch of things on your 'TO DO' list done." Jane, an "insult for insult" mate like Joe, might respond in many ways, two of which are:

Instant Insult Return

She might play the "silent" game awhile to punish Joe, or flee to another room to pout. She might hurl back an insult like, "Well! All you ever do is work, work, work! You don't care about me! You're married to your job! You're just like your father, Bill! I think I'll just call you 'Bill' from now on! Bill!!!"

Delayed Insult Return

Jane says to herself as she plots, "I'll be nice and forgiving to him now, but the next time he wants to get romantic, I'll put him in his place!"

She further plots in her mind, "Ah ha! He wants to visit his brother next weekend. Well, I'll be nice until the day we are to go and then I'll tell him I don't want to go, or that I'm not feeling well, or whatever will get him back for what he said! He'll think twice about insulting me next time!" "Insult for Insult" mates need to ask God to reveal the sin in their hearts such as unforgiveness, resentment, and bitterness.

Returning insults is a part of the devil's plan to isolate and destroy, creating a deep wedge in a couple's relationship. If this "Insult for Insult" cycle continues, the relationship will spiral down to destruction. Joe and Jane need to confess their self-centeredness to God and to one another.

The Lord desires us to receive our mates unconditionally and choose to return undeserved blessings, even when we don't feel like it. When this is done God will be honored in our marriage. Read 1 Peter 3:8-12; the central focus is verse nine:

"Do not repay evil with evil or insult with insult, but with blessing, because to this you were called so that you may inherit a blessing."

In the power of the Holy Spirit, we can choose to return blessings, rather than insults, by replying with gentle, quiet, understanding words that build, heal, and encourage. We also can choose to return blessings by demonstrating loving conduct, such as writing a tender note, providing a favorite meal by candlelight, or preparing a hot bath!

7. EMOTIONAL HOOK MATE

Usually due to parental modeling and conditioning when growing up as a child, this mate learns to get what is wanted by making loved ones (like a mate and children) feel guilty. Many do this without even knowing it. They learn to control family members by using improper, manipulative emotions. Others feel smothered; there is little peace in the home.

Example: Jack buys his wife a brand new sewing machine, just what she wanted! But wait! There's more! There's a lot more to this gift than meets the eye! Look! There are strings attached!

Yes, Jill loves the gift and now is made to feel that she owes it to Jack to allow him to go on his week-long fishing trip. This puts Jill in a bind. He "hooks" her. She has not been feeling well, being pregnant, and she is not sure she can take care of the household and care for their two small children if Jack is going to be gone for a whole week! Even though Jack does not say it out loud, with his body language, attitude, and "emotional hookery" he clearly communicates to Jill that she would be ungrateful if she did not give him her blessing to go on his trip.

If this "emotional hookery" is not stopped, in time, many other areas of their family relationships may be affected, such as sexual manipulation or making adult children feel guilty for not "coming home" more often. Their relationship may soon be "tumbling down the hill"!

8. CODEPENDENT MATE

This mate is in pain, emotional pain and possibly even physical pain. This mate is experiencing real pain because of making some very unhealthy choices regarding relationships.

The codependent mate would clearly disagree with this. She would say that she is trying as hard as she can to keep the marriage or family together. She would even go so far as to say that she is not trying hard enough!

A typical scenario goes something like this: A husband struggles in some area of his life such as alcoholism, over control, rage, physical or emotional abuse, gambling, lust, pornography, or some other addiction. Since he refuses to acknowledge that he even has a problem, the codependent mate, wanting to be valiant and oh so responsible, begins to assume responsibility for her mate.

She begins to believe that she is responsible for his problems. She must be the reason for his anger outbursts, sin, and other unresolved issues. If she does not feel responsible for causing his problems, then she usually feels that it is "on her shoulders" to correct, make better, heal, straighten out, or fix these problems. She is a rescuer and a helper. The more she tries to "fix" his sins or problems, the more he will "look at her" as the one who is responsible for it all.

This is why a codependent wife will tend to become an extension of her alcoholic husband's "very ill-very sinful" personality. She tends to lose her own identity. When he's up, she's up. When he's down, she's down. He, in his denial, refuses to own or face up to the fact that he has a very serious problem. He is in sin and blatant rebellion against God.

He tends to make her "the problem" or "the cause" of his drinking. He might say, "You drive me to drink!" She will believe him. She will take on the blame and become the martyr. She will, no doubt, feel guilty most of the time. Since she feels responsible, she runs herself ragged trying to be a better, nicer, more supportive, less nagging wife. Very few of her needs are getting met.

The truth is that this codependent thinking and rescuing type of behavior never works! In fact, it fuels the whole mess! She gets so frustrated and discouraged that she will lie for her husband, buy him liquor, and clean up his messes to try to appease him. In other words, she will enable him. She thinks, "What would happen if the neighbors or his boss found out?"

Deep down in her heart she feels if people found out, not only would her husband be looked down upon, but more important to her, she would be looked down upon. After all, she feels the whole mess is her fault and her responsibility! She feels she would look like a failure! "We shouldn't talk about this problem. We'll pretend there is NO PROBLEM!"

To be a part of the solution, she needs to continue to love her husband and realize that she is not responsible for her husband's sin addiction. She does not "drive him to drink"; he drives himself to drink.

She needs to firmly, reverently, and respectfully refuse to rescue him, cover for him, and lie for him, or in any way enable him in his destructive choices. If need be, he may need to lose his job and hit rock bottom before he begins to own responsibility for his life and actions.

This is "tough love." This brave lady will need encouragement and support if she is going to keep from sliding back into codependency. She could benefit greatly from a church group based on prayer and Scripture.

Satan will accuse her of not "gracing" and not loving her hurting husband. He will tempt her with thoughts like, "After all, doesn't the Bible tell wives to love, support, serve, and respect their husbands?"

Let me be clear! This wife will be loving, submitting to, respecting her husband and helping him the most if she:

- Gives up trying to be responsible for her husband's hurtful, sinful choices and lovingly insists that he be responsible for his own choices.
- Finds ways to affirm him and bless him as long as her choices don't feed or encourage his problems and sins.
- Is gentle and respectful.
- Prays for him and asks the Lord to help her break out of her codependency.
- Gets the help and support she desperately needs.
- Talks about the "problem" and doesn't bury it.

Although she is "one flesh" with her mate, she is to have her own separate healthy, growing identity in Christ.

She is to worship God and God alone. Codependency is sinful because it takes what is due God and gives it to man. It is clearly a sinful, destructive choice that disobeys and dishonors God and leads to the preoccupation of the soul not with God, but, instead, with people and self.

9. CONTROLLING MATE

This mate is so insecure that he ends up trying to control everyone in the family. He has to be at the center of all decision making and usually is at the center of tension and conflict in the home.

Instead of serving, leading, or encouraging, he controls. Again this mate probably learned this controlling technique from observing a controlling parent. He is, however, without excuse. He stands alone before God.

He may use shame, guilt, sarcasm, or rage. He controls by use of moods and temper. Sometimes just "that look" will get other controlled family members to "shape up" or else! They feel they must "walk on eggshells" whenever he is around.

He may puff up like a blow fish when things are not going his way. He may get angry, his eyes may widen, his jaw may tighten, and he may try to become bigger than he really is. He may even overeat and gain weight to wield more power. You see, he needs to get bigger to try to compensate for how terribly small he feels inside.

Sometimes a controlling husband will spiritually abuse family members. He might command his wife to do or not do certain things all in the name of headship and submission. Then he might inflict the cruelest type of guilt upon his wife by telling her that God will punish her if she does not obey him. He might also abuse her or other family members by dredging up past times when they have failed or sinned. This is the devil's way.

It is important for a wife to set boundaries and limits on what she will tolerate from a controlling mate.

She must firmly confront him on his destructive attitudes and behaviors, and let him know what consequences there will be to any abusive behavior. (such as him having to leave the house, reporting him to the Elders of the church, or simply calling the police) Then she must be sure to follow through. It would also be wise to get help from a pastor, biblical counselor, or police if necessary.

10. TWO-FACED MATE

This mate is moody and seems to be always on somebody's "case" at home. She may yell or brood or hold grudges. While at home (or with the private family) she seems like the furthest thing from being a Christian. There is little mercy, little forbearance, and a lot of accusation. She is self-focused.

Once she steps out of the house and mingles at church, at a Bible study, at work, or at a party, she instantly transforms herself into "The Public Princess." She is nice, tenderhearted, and a good listener. The "perfect" Christian! No one would believe what she is like once back at home.

Her mate is frustrated! The children are confused! They wonder, "Who is our real mom?" Their understanding of a true Christian is greatly hindered. Will the real mom please step forward? Only one face is needed. And may Christ be the One who shines through that one face!

11. SHAMING MATE

This mate, although a child of God, feels he has to earn God's love by being a good citizen and going to church, at least more than the "Jones." He tries to appease what he believes to be an angry, hard-to-please God. He believes a lie!

He feels like he has to measure up to an impossible set of standards. Most likely, he feels he had to earn this kind of approval from his parents and, sad to say, possibly even from his church, which might have been legalistic or performance-based. (The more you do for us, the better you should feel and the more we'll like you!) Therefore he measures his mate's performance by the same legalistic standard he has imposed on himself.

The shaming mate seldom affirms, praises, or encourages his mate. He feels, "Why should I? My mate doesn't deserve it!"

The "shaming" mate feels "stuck" or even "sentenced" to live out his life with his mate. This "shaming" mate tends to belittle, ridicule, and tear down his mate.

Through words, attitude, body language, or priorities, the "shaming" mate communicates that his mate:

- Is not good enough.
- Needs to improve to earn favor and love.
- Simply does not measure up.
- Is flawed, was a mistake to marry, and now has to be tolerated.

The mate being shamed feels like there is always something wrong with who she is. She feels flawed, permanently unacceptable! She believes that she just can't "measure up" to be the kind of person the shaming mate wants or demands her to be. She assumes God also rejects her in this manner. Shame is not the name of the game!

12. CHRISTIAN MATE CONTROLLED BY THE FLESH

(See Galatians Chapter 5)

This mate, either out of ignorance or rebellion, chooses to run her life in her own way. She wants God and others to revolve around her own goals and dreams. Even though Jesus has saved her, she refuses to let Him "empower and direct" her life. She tries to live the Christian life without appropriating the power and love of the Holy Spirit who lives within her. Fatigue, frustration, and misery are inevitable. Only Jesus can live the Christian life. He wants to live this "abundant life" (John 10:10) in and through her, but she refuses to surrender or yield.

Her independence from God opens the door to other sins such as worry, fear, impatience, anger, resentment, ambition, idolatry, grudge-holding and immorality. The harder she tries to live right, the greater will be the struggle. Her marriage and family suffer! Satan is pleased! She thinks she is in control, but she is fooled by Satan and is actually out of control. This is not what God wants. This is sin!

Wave Calmers

1. CHRISTIAN MATE CONTROLLED BY THE HOLY SPIRIT (See Galatians Chapter 5)

This wise mate has found that the key to the Christian life is not struggle but surrender! This mate wants what Jesus wants for her life more than what she wants for her life. (Job 22:21)

She desires God's Holy Spirit to fill, direct, control, and empower her life. By faith, she will go throughout the day depending on the Lord. She recognizes that yielding to God is an hour by hour, minute by minute choice.

She is sensitive to the conviction of the Holy Spirit when she does allow self to be in control. She responds by confessing her sin and yielding to the Lord, asking the Holy Spirit to once again control, direct, and empower her life by faith.

She chooses not to shame, insult, manipulate, or nag her mate or children since these "choices" would be sin and would be acts indicative of the flesh that wants to take command!

Her life will show the Spirit's fruit. Galatians 5:22 says:

"But the fruit of the Spirit is love, joy, peace, patience, kindness, goodness, faithfulness, gentleness and self-control...."

This Spirit-controlled Christian desires this fruit to develop in her life in order to bring glory to God.

2. SUFFERING MATE

(Special Note: The Suffering Mate is not a role or a choice that someone adopts. Unless the suffering is resulting from sin, the family suffering does not have a choice. Suffering is a part of life. How an individual or family **responds to suffering** and pain will ultimately determine if the marriage partners involved will drift apart or be drawn close together and to the Lord.) The following Scripture refers to Jesus and His personal growth:

"Although he was a son, he learned obedience from what he suffered." (Hebrews 5:8)

The Suffering Mate may feel that no one understands what he is experiencing. He has gone through terrible times! His heart is filled with tears that still have not been shed.

He may have suffered the loss of a dearly beloved family member or friend. He or a loved one might be suffering pain and fear from enduring a long, dismal battle with cancer, AIDS, MS, heart failure, or some other medical problem. Perhaps he struggles with depression, or faces difficulties at home, work, or church. Perhaps he is grieving because of an unfaithful mate. It is possible other church members have judged him and set him aside.

Turtle? Porcupine?

He may respond like a turtle and then a porcupine. Because the trauma or illness in his life is ever present, it will serve as a mean, ruthless club!

The pain and tension will beat him mercilessly. He may be drained, wiped out, and weary. He may feel 10, 15, or even 20 years older than he is. Migraine headaches, digestive problems, and overeating may occur. Sleeping problems are common.

Dangers!

One of the dangers the Suffering Mate faces is that of retreating emotionally. Like the turtle, he may hide inside his shell, building up a wall of isolation. He may distance himself from loved ones and pour himself into his work. He may be a prime candidate for an affair. Another danger is that the suffering mate may radiate emotional pain almost like there is an invisible circle of pain surrounding him. In addition to retreating like a turtle, he may now send out painful emotional barbs like a porcupine.

Here it seems to be true that the suffering mate hurts most the ones he loves most. The family members being hurt are simply in the suffering mate's circle of pain. If both mates are suffering, and they usually are, each mate in each other's "porcupine barb range" gets barbed quite often.

Needed: The Gift of Understanding

This hurting mate is crying out for someone to understand him. He doesn't need words that tell him, "Oh just wait! Things will get better soon! Aunt Tilly had that and she's doing fine now." or "Well, you messed up years ago. You're done as far as serving the Lord goes. You're on the shelf."

No! What he needs is understanding. He wants people to cry with him and just sit quietly with him or go for a walk with him. He needs loyal friends to enter into his world of pain and tell him things like, "Tom, what you are going through must be awful. How you must hurt. There's not much I can say but I just want to be with you. I care for you."

Needed: Awareness and Encouragement

These suffering mates need to be aware of these symptoms and dangers, and they should not be hesitant to ask others for help through their difficult time. They need kindness, understanding, think-time, and good friends who will shoot straight with them if need be. They need to realize that the pain they are experiencing is real and that others are in pain also. This will help them stop the "blame game" or the "poor me" game if they are tempted to play them.

They may need to forgive others and release all to God. Praying, walking, talking, and having some fun are all helpful. They are not alone in their struggle! The Lord understands! Godly character is forged and obedience is learned through suffering. If eyes are on Christ, many good things can result. The key is keeping your eyes on Christ and getting the help you need.

3. PARENT-HONORING MATES

In Exodus 20:12, God speaks the following words:

"Honor your father and your mother so that you may live long in the land the Lord your God is giving you."

Today we hear much about assigning blame to our parents for all of the struggles, hang-ups and weaknesses that we now face. If we can just understand our past, the way we were raised and the "wrong choices" our parents made in raising us, then we can "rightfully" place blame on them and somehow we will then feel better. Then we can blame them for our foolish, irresponsible living.

This, however, is very destructive! This blaming of our parents, grandparents, and in-laws leads to resentment, pride, and despair. However, looking appropriately at our past and our family experience in order to see some of the foundational causes of our problems is beneficial.

Forgiveness is required. Owning our own adult choices and being accountable to God are also mandatory. We stand alone before God.

When we understand the framework and dynamics of our struggles and strongholds, they begin to lose power over us. They begin to lose their grip on our private lives. Wisdom can break these chains, allowing the light of Christ to enlighten, heal, and free us.

Whatever we do, let us not blame our parents! Instead we need to bestow grace and mercy upon them. We need to thank God for them even if they hurt us deeply. You see, we are to forgive as God has forgiven us. "*Forgive as the Lord forgave you.*" (Colossians 3:13b) Grudge-holding, bitterness, and being stuck in your past will accomplish nothing and will waste your life.

Parent Honoring Mates will understand that their parents did a good job in many areas of raising them as well as falling short in other areas. In most cases, parents do the best they can with what resources and knowledge they have. These mates realize that, apart from God's kindness and grace, they would easily fall and probably do a poorer job at marriage and parenting than their parents. Parent-Honoring Mates will be committed to what God desires and that is that they honor their parents. Treat them as if they were the parents God had hoped they would be.

Two sides to every coin

Just as there are two sides to every coin, there are also two sides to honoring parents and in-laws:

Honor: Side One

Make it a point to genuinely revere your parents and be thankful for them. Don't forget, it was God who chose them for you.

"Grace" them. You are to grace and bless them because God graces and blesses you every hour of every day. Also He commands you to honor them (Exodus 20:12). Forgive them if forgiveness is needed. Hold them in high regard.

You might honor your parents with a tribute by writing on paper what they mean to you. This is an opportunity to thank them and appreciate them. Have it framed. It is a gift they would always treasure.

Honor: Side Two

This side requires you to spend time on your knees in prayer before God. You see, many Parent Honoring Mates have parents who are either not Christians or who simply do not approve of or respect their adult married children's values, convictions, interpretation of the Bible, or their life style.

Some have parents who try to manipulate (emotional hookery), who use shame and ridicule, placing demands on them. Some parents may give generously, but subtly have strings attached. Some, with sweet, poisonous words, will attempt to cause friction in their children's marriages. Sometimes they will want to maintain control.

Parent-Honoring Mates may have to confront the offending in-laws or parents. This should always be done with reverence and respect. Going to an offending, abusive, or shame-oriented parents' house alone may be too threatening and damaging to their own marriage. They may need to go together.

The Parent-Honoring Mates are not to judge them, give lengthy or repetitive explanations, or be disrespectful. They are to be kind, loving, and very firm! If they are not firm and decisive here, Satan will use their parents to cause division and the "taking of sides" in their marriage. Make no mistake about it! If these problems are not dealt with, they can destroy a marriage.

It is painful. Parents may throw everything in their arsenal at their married children. They may accuse them. They may try to somehow punish them. They may even threaten to disown them. They probably won't understand. Remember: They don't need to.

With loving kindness and firm gentleness, the Parent-Honoring Mates will stick to their convictions and decisions. It will not seem or feel like they are bringing honor to their parents, but they are.

"Therefore what God has joined together, let man not separate." (Mark 10:9)

"Man" includes parents and in-laws!

Special Note:

Unless there are crimes or immoral behaviors in your children's grandparents' home, please do not withhold your children from them. This is cruel. Your kids need their grandparents even though you may not fully agree on every issue of life.

4. SUBMISSION

To submit is to voluntarily come under the authority of someone; to reverently and respectfully look out for the other's best interests.

It does not mean that you serve as a "doormat" or a "slave." It does not mean that you should obey a mate who is sinning overtly, obviously, or blindly against God and you.

If your husband is establishing a pattern of disobedience and rebellion against the Lord, and he is asking you to do likewise, or to endorse his sin, or to cover for him, ask God to help you determine what words and actions on your part would be best for your husband's spiritual welfare.

God will help you deal with your husband properly. Timing, patience, and honesty are important. You may need to tenderly confront him. You are his helpmate. If you don't help him see his sin, who will?

Love and respect him, but do not fall into the trap of condoning or being a party to his sin and foolishness. God does not take aiding and abetting sin lightly.

5. TOUGH LOVE

This is loving action that goes against the tide of sin and irresponsibility, such as in alcohol abuse, continued physical abuse, and unrepentant adultery. Tough love does not feed someone's sin. It starves the sin.

Example: If your husband is an alcoholic who, instead of being wise in his weakness, remains foolish, you may need to reverently, respectfully, and firmly refuse to rescue or enable him.

With a spirit of firm, determined gentleness (tough love), you may need to let him experience the full consequences of his foolish, sinful, and destructive choices. Many alcoholics will live in denial until reality is allowed to come crashing in. This is also often true of those who are in bondage to other sin addictions.

If you "soft love" him by always rescuing him, cleaning up after him, lying to cover for him regarding his job and church, you won't be loving him at all!

You certainly won't be looking out for his "best interests." You will, on the other hand, be enabling him in his irresponsibility and in his sin. In "soft love" everyone loses. The "soft lover" who ends up enabling and, in reality, promoting her husband's hurtful attitudes and behaviors will also experience damage to her emotions.

Tough Love always has restoration, godly character, and strengthening of the marriage as its goal.

Tough love honors God, and is committed to oneness in marriage.

6. GRACING MATE

This mate receives gratefully the Lord's love, forgiveness, and unmerited favor. He understands that he is made righteous by Christ's substitutionary death on the cross and His victorious resurrection. He does not have to earn it.

He embraces the truth that he is totally and forever accepted by God. He is thankful that because of this, he is the apple of God's eye. He knows as fact that he is forever in God's family! Nothing in the universe can ever shake or alter this eternal truth to those who love Christ.

Wanting to model God's amazing love and blessing, he will look upon his mate with thanksgiving. As a gracing mate he will bestow unmerited favor upon her. He will love, accept, and delight in her, regardless of performance. He will be kind and gentle. The receiving mate of such grace will tend to feel loved, affirmed, and valued. She will tend to feel free from the tyranny and bondage of having to improve, measure up, earn approval, or meet standards of performance. By God's grace, she will want to grow spiritually, pleasing and reverencing God and her "gracing" mate.

Ideally, God's desire is that both mates grace and affirm each other. However, whether or not the other mate "graces" back, the "gracing" mate will continue to "grace" with reverence, respect, and tough, steadfast love.

A Quiet Place for You to Journal

Today's date: ______________________________

Jot down your thoughts, feelings, hurts, joys, ups and downs. Just be yourself. Perhaps write to the Lord Jesus something on your heart only He would understand. Maybe jot down a prayer request that only God could answer.

Today's date: ______________________

Pour your heart out before the Lord Jesus. Tell Him like it really is. Tell Him your pain, your joy, your disappointment, and your dreams for the future. Then give Him all of your heart and life… all of it. Fully surrender. Capture your thoughts and feelings on the lines below. (Psalm 62:8)

Today's date: ______________________________

Take some moments to hide. Find a quiet place, a closet, a soft chair, a warm couch by the fire, or a gentle, wooded glade. Go there with Jesus, and your Bible. Just be still before Him. He dearly loves you. Tell Him what is stirring in your heart. Read some Scripture. Then quietly listen to Him. Let Him cradle and comfort you. (Zephaniah 3:17)

Today's date: ______________________________

Practice the presence of your Lord Jesus Christ. He is with you always. As best you can, give Him the things that are tugging at you. Give Him everything that bothers you and causes sadness, aloneness, and pain. He is pursuing you and He is listening. Perhaps do this together with your mate or fiancé. Completely sign over all rights to your life in full surrender to the Lord. **Sign** your names below and date it after you both have done so.

His: ______________________ Date: __________

Hers: ______________________ Date: __________

Today's date: ______________________________

Write down two character qualities your mate/fiancé possesses that you are thankful for. Then write a few words of gratitude to God for fashioning those qualities in him/her.

Today's date: ______________________________

Please find a good moment to share these two qualities with your mate/fiancé. Jot down his/her response and how you felt after sharing. (Hebrews 3:13)

Today's date: ______________________________

Write down exactly how you feel right now. If faith is choosing to live as though the Bible is true, regardless of circumstances, emotions, and cultural trends, how will living by faith affect your thinking and possibly your feelings? (Romans 12:2)

Today's date: ______________________________

If today were the last day you and your mate/fiancé would be on earth, what adjustments would you make in how you treat each other right now? (Ephesians 4:32)

Today's date: ____________________

How will the principle, "What is best for your marriage, will be best for your family, work, and church" affect your children if God gives them to you?

Today's date: ______________________________

How will the principle, "What is best for your marriage, will be best for your family, work, and church" affect your in-laws? Also jot down the low point and the high point of the last 4 or 5 days. Any connection is purely coincidental.

Today's date: ____________________

Take a few moments now to seek the face of the Lord and be utterly still before Him. Just rest in His presence. Do not talk. Just rest and let Him be God in your life. Write down what this experience is like for you today. (Exodus 33:14)

Today's date: ______________________________

Read a passage of Scripture and identify a key verse that is helpful to you. Write down that verse below and share how it helps you today.

Today's date: ______________________________

Write down the things that originally drew you to your mate / fiancé. Have you forgotten to thank God for those things? If you focus on where your mate is winning or even partially winning, how will this bless your relationship?

Today's date: ______________________________

Tell the Lord your deepest hopes, dreams, and desires today. He is close and wants to hear every word. He loves you so much and will help you. Journal your thoughts, insights, and feelings.

Today's date: ______

In desiring for your marriage to be a light shining across the dark and stormy sea or the lantern showing the way in a dark forest, how might others be strengthened and encouraged by your commitment to this objective?

Start a Group Study!

To order books for your group study contact:

New Life Resources
Campus Crusade for Christ
Attn: Pat Pearce, Executive Director
375 Highway 74 South, Suite A
Peachtree City, GA 30269

Toll Free: 1-800-827-2788

Web (Public): http://www.campuscrusade.com/RTRB
(CCC Staff Only): http://staff.campuscrusade.org/RTRB

Email: nlrrep@campuscrusade.com

OR

Jim & Barbara Grunseth
Email: jgrunseth@centurytel.net

If you need assistance and insight blending families, please contact us. Let us help you bring peace and joy to your family.

—Jim & Barb Grunseth